The All-Year-Long Songbook

Compiled by ROSLYN RUBIN
and JUDY WATHEN

Woodcuts by WHITNEY HANSEN

SCHOLASTIC BOOK SERVICES
NEW YORK · TORONTO · LONDON · AUCKLAND · SYDNEY · TOKYO

To Dr. Jerome Green, Principal, P.S. 111.
— R.R.

With grateful acknowledgment
to Martha Parlitsis, Judy Gorman,
and all the other people on the
Scholastic staff who worked
so hard to produce this book.
And special thanks to
Irwin Rabinowitz.

ISBN: 0-590-30962-5

12 11 10 9 8 7 6 5 4 3 2 1   1   1 2 3 4 5/8

Printed in the U.S.A.   10

Contents

School

Finger Plays and Singing Games

Rhythms

Autumn and Halloween

Indians and Thanksgiving

Hanukkah and Christmas

Winter

Winter Holidays

Spring

Transportation

Animals

Circus

Other Lands

School

Good Morning

Moderately

"Good morn - ing!" says the sun. "A hap - py day to you!" And
lit - tle chil - dren here in school may say "Good morn - ing," too.

Everybody Come

Ev-'ry-bod-y come ev-'ry day. Ev-'ry-bod-y come ev-'ry day.
We_____ skip and run and we have a lot of fun,
So_____ ev-'ry-bod-y come ev-'ry day.

Here We Are Together

1. Here we are to-geth-er, to-geth-er, to-geth-er,
Oh, here we are to-geth-er, to-geth-er at school.

We'll all learn to read and we'll all learn to write,—

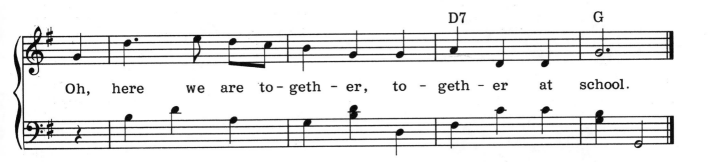

Oh, here we are to-geth-er, to-geth-er at school.

2. The more we get together, together, together,
   The more we get together, the happier
     we'll be.
   For your friends are my friends, and my
     friends are your friends,
   The more we get together, the happier
     we'll be.

Have children make up additional verses. (E.g., "We'll learn
how to sing, and we'll learn how to dance..."; "We'll all eat
our lunch, then we'll go out to play..."; etc.)

Mary Wore a Red Dress

Lively

Mar - y wore a red dress, a red dress, a red dress.—

Mar - y wore a red dress—— all day long.

This is a good song for getting acquainted. Children can make up additional verses about members of the class. (E.g., "Johnny wore a blue shirt..."; "Sally wore her green socks..."; etc.)

Today Is Monday

Lively

To-day is Mon - day,— To-day is Mon - day,— Mon-day String beans,

All you hun-gry chil-dren, Come and eat it up. To-day is Tues-day,— To-day is

Tues - day,— Tues-day Spa-ghet - ti, Mon-day String beans, All you hun-gry

chil-dren, Come and eat it up. To-day is Come and eat it up.—

3. Today is Wednesday, today is Wednesday
   Wednesday, ZOOOOP
   Tuesday, spaghetti,
   Monday, string beans
   All you hungry children
   Come and eat it up.

4. Today is Thursday, today is Thursday
   Thursday, roast beef
   Wednesday, ZOOOOP, etc.

5. Today is Friday, today is Friday
   Friday, fresh fish, etc.

6. Today is Saturday, today is Saturday
   Saturday, chicken, etc.

7. Today is Sunday, today is Sunday
   Sunday, ice cream, etc.

Tick-Tock

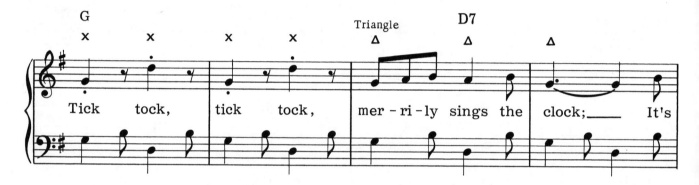

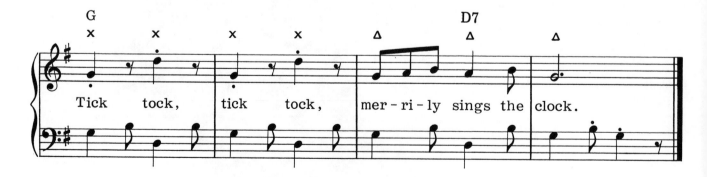

Words and music by Richard C. Berg. From MUSIC FOR YOUNG AMERICANS © 1966. Reprinted by permission of American Book Company.

Put-Away Time

Moderately

1., 2. Oh, it's put-a-way time, Oh, it's put-a-way time,
1. Pick up your blocks and put them on the shelf,
2. Pick up your toys and put them in the box,

1., 2. Oh, it's put-a-way time, Oh, it's put-a-way time,
1. Put all your blocks on the shelf.
2. Put all your toys in the box.

Improvise additional verses for other activities throughout
the day. (E.g., "Oh, it's time for juice...wash your hands
and come to the table"; "Oh, it's going-home time...zip up
your leggins and put on your coats"; etc.)

Hot and Cold Water

Moderately

Wa - ter that's hot, wa - ter that's cold,

They're not the same, need you be told?

If you can spell, then you will see,

C - O - L - D or H - O - T;

Don't turn the fau - cet un - til you have looked, Un -

less you have fin - gers that like to be cooked;

Words and music by Irving Caesar and Gerald Marks. © Irving Caesar. © Marlong Music Pub. Co. Reprinted by permission.

Safety

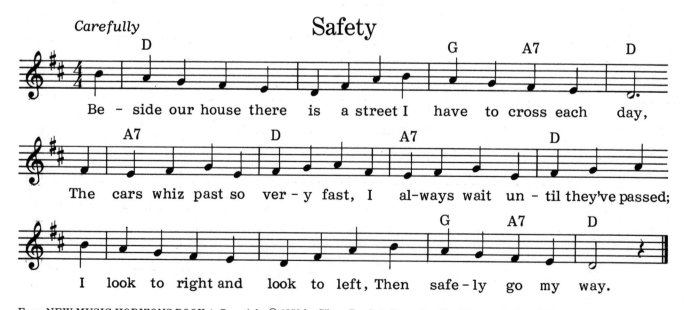

Carefully

Be - side our house there is a street I have to cross each day,

The cars whiz past so ver - y fast, I al - ways wait un - til they've passed;

I look to right and look to left, Then safe - ly go my way.

What Shall We Do When We All Go Out?

Rhythmically

1. What shall we do when we all go out, All go out, all go out,
2. We'll ride our bikes when we all go out, All go out, all go out,

What shall we do when we all go out, All go out to play?
We'll ride our bikes when we all go out, All go out to play.

3. We'll skip rope when we all go out, etc.
4. We'll play ball, etc.
5. We'll play train, etc.
6. We'll fly planes, etc.

Finger Plays and Singing Games

Ten Green Apples

Moderately

D — A7 — D

1. Farm-er Brown had ten green ap-ples hang-ing on a tree.
2. Farm-er Brown had nine (etc.)

A7 — D

Farm-er Brown had ten green ap-ples hang-ing on a tree. Then he

G — D — A — D — G

plucked one ap-ple and he ate it greed-i-ly, Leav-ing nine green ap-ples_ a-
(eight)

D — A7 — D — *instr.* — G — D — A7 — D

hang-ing on a tree.

Have children continue the song until there are "no green apples a-hanging on a tree."

"Ten Green Apples" by Alan Mills used by permission of Mrs. G. L. Miller and Folkways Records. NY. © 1972.

Ten in the Bed

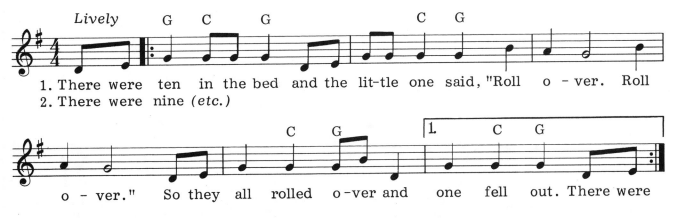

1. There were ten in the bed and the lit-tle one said, "Roll o - ver. Roll
2. There were nine (etc.)

o - ver." So they all rolled o - ver and one fell out. There were

Continue the countdown until: "There was one in the bed and
the little one said, 'GOOD NIGHT!' "

This Old Man

Lively

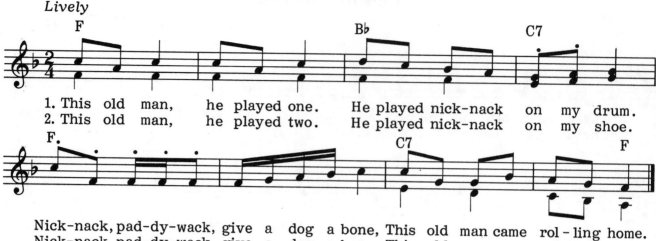

1. This old man, he played one. He played nick-nack on my drum.
2. This old man, he played two. He played nick-nack on my shoe.

Nick-nack, pad-dy-wack, give a dog a bone, This old man came rol-ling home.
Nick-nack, pad-dy-wack, give a dog a bone, This old man came rol-ling home.

three...knee
four...door (or floor)
five...hive
six...sticks (or chicks)

seven...Heaven
eight...gate (or plate)
nine...spine
ten...hen (or—now let's sing this song again)

Ten Little Fingers

Briskly

I have ten lit-tle fin-gers and they all be-long to me!

I can make them do things, Would you like to see?

I can shut them up tight Or o-pen them wide, I can

hold them in front Or make them all hide; I can hold them up high, I can

put them down low; I can hide them in back, Then hold them just so!

From FINGER PLAY by Mary Miller and Paula Zajan. Copyright © 1955 by G. Schirmer, Inc. Used by permission of G. Schirmer, Inc.

Two Little Eyes

Clearly

Two lit-tle eyes that | o-pen and close; | Two lit-tle ears and | one lit-tle nose;

Two lit-tle cheeks and | one lit-tle chin; | Two lit-tle lips with the | teeth closed in!

Two little eyes that open and close,

Two little ears

and one little nose,

Two little cheeks

and one little chin,

Two little lips with the teeth closed in!

From FINGER PLAY by Mary Miller and Paula Zajan. Copyright © 1955 by G. Schirmer, Inc. Used by permission of G. Schirmer, Inc.

Where Is Thumbkin?

Where is Thumbkin?

Here I am.

How are you this morning? *Wiggle right thumb.*
Very well. I thank you. *Wiggle left thumb.*

Run away.

2. Pointer 3. Tall Man 4. Ringman 5. Pinky 6. All Men

Eency Weency Spider

Steadily

Een - cy ween - cy spi - der went up the wa - ter spout;

Down came the rain and washed the spi - der out.

Out came the sun and dried up all the rain,

And the een - cy, ween - cy spi - der went up the spout a - gain.

Eency weency spider
went up the water spout.

Thumb to pointer.
Pointer to thumb.

Continue repeating.

Down came the rain

Raise hands up and down,
wiggling fingers.

and washed the spider out.

Push hands away from body,
palms out.

Out came the sun
and dried up all the rain.

Raise arms in a circle around
head and smile.

And the eency weency spider
went up the spout again.

Repeat first action.

I'm a Little Teapot

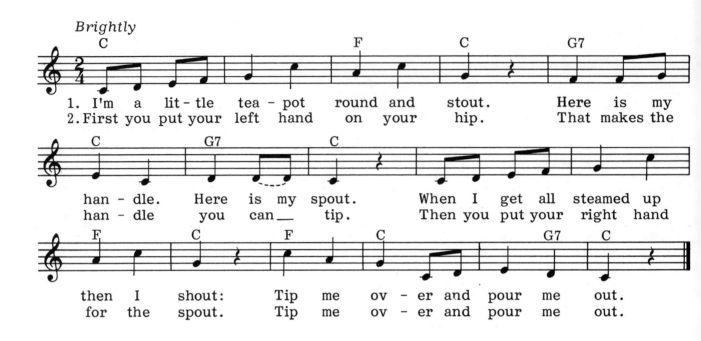

Left to the Window

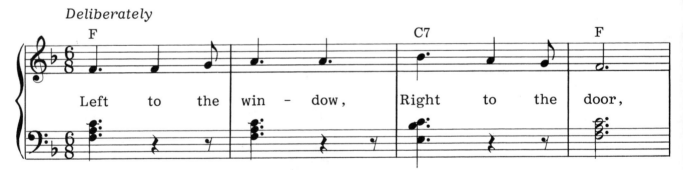

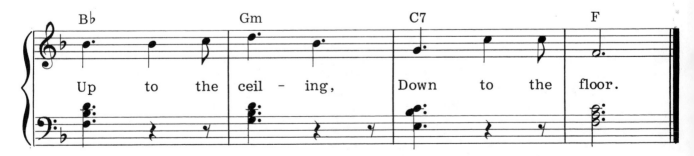

Put Your Finger in the Air

Moderately

1. Put your fin-ger in the air,— in the air. Put your fin-ger in the air,— in the air. Put your fin-ger in the air and leave it a-bout a year. Put your fin-ger in the air,— in the air.———

2. Put your finger on your head...tell me is it
   green or red?
3. cheek...leave it there about a week.
4. nose...is that where the cold wind blows?
5. chest...give it just a little rest.
6. belly...make it shake like apple jelly.

Encourage children to make up other verses, such as: "Put
your finger on your shoulder...and leave it till you're older."

Use the same tune to sing "If You're Happy and You Know It
Clap Your Hands (clap, clap)." Additional verses: tap your
toe, nod your head, do all three, touch your nose, snap your
fingers, sit real still, etc.

Stamping Land

Rhythmically

1. I trav-eled far a - cross the sea. I met a man and old was he. "Old man," I said, "Where do you live?" And this is what he told me: "Fol - low me to stamp-ing land, stamp-ing land, stamp-ing land. All who wish to live with me, fol - low me to stamp-ing land."

2. clapping land
3. skipping land
4. pointing land
5. nodding land

6. hopping land
7. tapping land
8. snapping land

Have children perform hand or body movements as the song suggests.

Get Into the Game

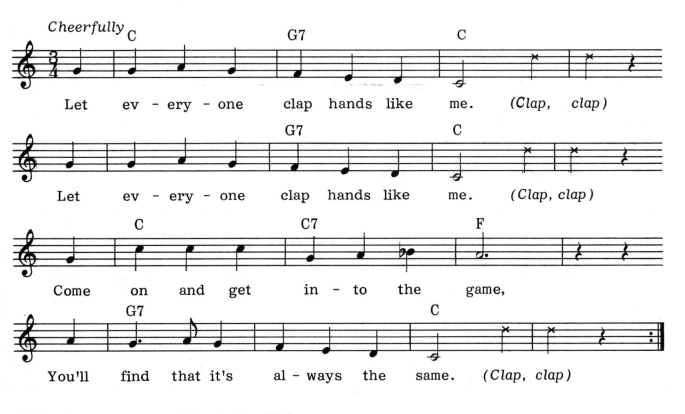

Let ev-ery-one clap hands like me. *(Clap, clap)*

Let ev-ery-one clap hands like me. *(Clap, clap)*

Come on and get in-to the game,

You'll find that it's al-ways the same. *(Clap, clap)*

Additional verses: tap toes, shake hands, whistle, etc.

B-I-N-G-O

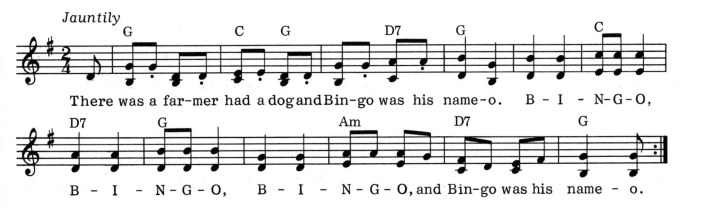

There was a far-mer had a dog and Bin-go was his name-o. B - I - N-G-O,

B - I - N-G-O, B - I - N - G-O, and Bin-go was his name - o.

Sing the verse through one time. The second time, substitute a clap for the letter "B." (E.g., "Clap-I-N-G-O.") In each succeeding verse substitute a clap for the next letter until the fifth time around, when you will have five "claps" replacing all five letters.

Do Your Ears Hang Low?

Playfully

Do your ears hang low? Do they
wob - ble to and fro? Can you tie them in a knot? Can you
tie them in a bow? Can you throw them o-ver your shoul-ders? Can you
pluck a mer - ry tune? Do your ears hang low?

From SALLY GO ROUND THE SUN by Edith Fowke. Reprinted by permission of The Canadian Publishers, McClelland and Stewart Limited, Toronto.

The If Song

Rhythmically

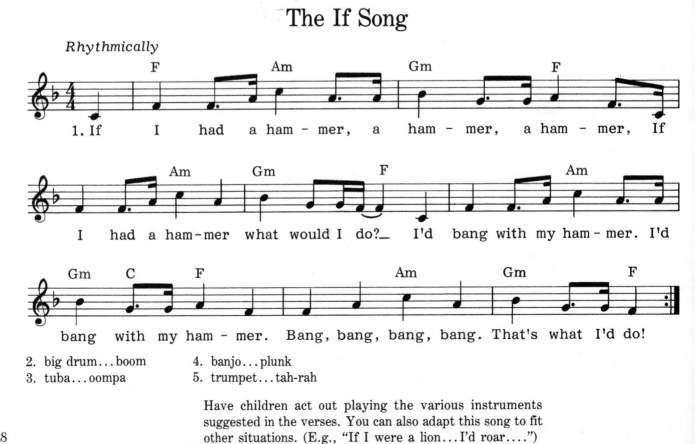

1. If I had a ham - mer, a ham - mer, a ham - mer, If
I had a ham-mer what would I do?_ I'd bang with my ham-mer. I'd
bang with my ham - mer. Bang, bang, bang, bang. That's what I'd do!

2. big drum...boom   4. banjo...plunk
3. tuba...oompa   5. trumpet...tah-rah

Have children act out playing the various instruments suggested in the verses. You can also adapt this song to fit other situations. (E.g., "If I were a lion...I'd roar....")

Hey, Betty Martin!

Hey, Bet-ty Mar-tin, tip-py toe, tip-py toe, Hey, Bet-ty Mar-tin, tip toe fine.

Hey, Bet-ty Mar-tin, tip-py toe, tip-py toe, Hey, Bet-ty Mar-tin, please be mine.

Skip with me, I'll skip with you, We'll go skip-ping the whole day through.

Skip so fine, skip so fine, Skip-ping, skip-ping all the time.

The beginning and end of this song should be sung and played softly for tiptoeing. The middle part is louder. In this middle part the movement may be changed from skipping to clapping, dancing, jumping, hopping, or bouncing.

Shoo Fly

Briskly

Shoo, fly don't both-er me. Shoo, fly don't both-er me.

Shoo, fly don't both-er me. For I be-long to some-bod - y.

I feel, I feel, I feel, I feel like a morn-ing star. I

feel, I feel, I feel, I feel, I feel like a morn-ing star. So

Have pairs of children join hands and form a circle. On the first line of the song, children march forward to the center of the circle, raising their hands above their heads as they march. On the next line of the song, children march backward to their original position, lowering their hands as they march. Repeat for the next two lines.

On the first "I feel, I feel, I feel" phrase, children lock righ elbows with their partners and march around each othe clockwise. On the next "I feel, I feel" phrase, children loc left elbows with their partners and march around each othe counterclockwise. It should work out that for the next vers children will have a new partner.

She'll Be Coming 'Round the Mountain

Brightly

Toot!

G

1. She'll be com-ing 'round the moun-tain when she comes.____

Toot! ____

Toot! D7

She'll be com-ing 'round the moun-tain when she comes.____

Toot! ____

G C

She'll be com-ing 'round the moun-tain, She'll be com-ing 'round the

G D7 G **Toot! Toot!**

moun-tain, She'll be com-ing 'round the moun-tain when she comes.____

2. She'll be driving six white horses when she
   comes. (Whoa, back!), etc.
3. Oh, we'll all go out to meet her when she
   comes. (Hi, babe!), etc.
4. Oh, we'll all have chicken and dumplings when
   she comes. (Yum, yum!), etc.

Hokey Pokey

Brightly

G

1. You put your right foot in, You put your right foot out.
2. You put your left foot in, You put your left foot out.

You put your right foot in and you shake it all a-bout.
You put your left foot in and you shake it all a-bout.

D7

And then you do the ho-key po-key, and you turn your-self a-bout.

G

And that's what it's all a - bout! Hey!

3. right hand
4. left hand
5. right shoulder
6. left shoulder

7. right hip
8. left hip
9. whole self

Bluebird

Gently

B♭

1. Blue - bird, blue - bird, on ____ my ____ win - dow,
2. Take a lit - tle {boy,}{girl,} tap {him}{her} on the shoul - der,

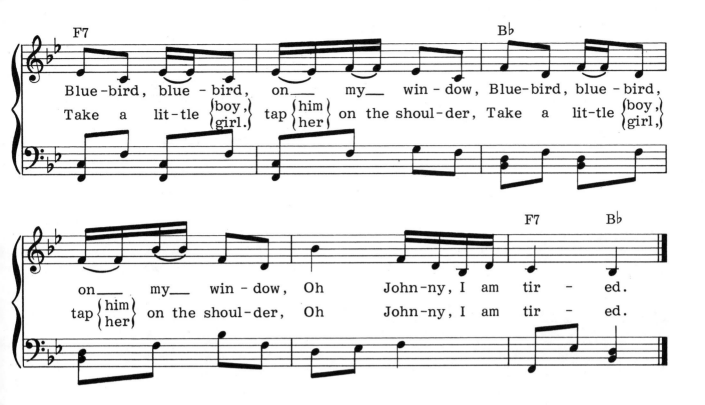

Have children stand in a circle. Pick one child to be the Bluebird and have that child stand outside the circle. The rest of the children join hands and raise their arms up to form arches.

On the first verse, the Bluebird weaves in and out through the arches with a skipping step.

On the second verse, the Bluebird stops behind one child and taps him or her on the shoulder in time to the music. At the end of the verse, the Bluebird places his hands on the shoulders of this *second* Bluebird.

The song is now repeated with the two Bluebirds weaving in and out through the arches, the second Bluebird leading. At the repeat of verse 2, a third Bluebird is chosen and the three Bluebirds weave through. The game continues until there are only two children remaining to form an arch and these become the first two Bluebirds of the next game.

On the very last time through the song, children sing the first verse, gradually decreasing the tempo, yawning and pantomiming fatigue. At the final line, "Oh, Johnny, I am tired," children collapse in a heap on the floor and pretend to sleep.

Aiken Drum

Fast

1. There__ was a man lived in the moon, lived
2. And his hat was made of good cream cheese, of

in the moon, lived in the moon, There__ was a man lived
good cream cheese, of good cream cheese, And his hat was made of

in the moon, and his name was Ai - ken Drum.
good cream cheese, and his name was Ai - ken Drum.

And he played up on a la - dle, a la - dle, a la - dle, And he

played up on a la - dle, and his name was Ai - ken Drum.

3. And his coat was made of good roast beef, etc.
4. And his buttons made of penny loaves, etc.
5. And his breeches made of haggis bags, etc.

Have children make up additional verses.

From THE FIRESIDE BOOK OF CHILDREN'S SONGS by Marie Winn and Allan Miller. Copyright © 1966 by Marie Winn and Allan Miller. Used by permission of Simon & Schuster, a Division of Gulf & Western Corporation.

Nobody Likes Me

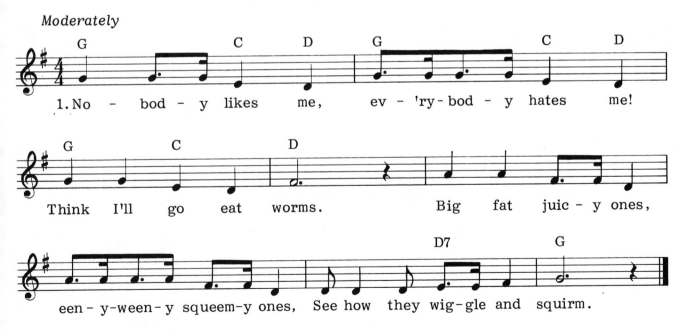

Moderately

1. No - bod - y likes me, ev - 'ry-bod - y hates me! Think I'll go eat worms. Big fat juic - y ones, een - y-ween - y squeem-y ones, See how they wig-gle and squirm.

2. Chop up their heads and squeeze out their juice
   And throw their tails away.
   Nobody knows how I survive
   On worms three times a day.

From SALLY GO ROUND THE SUN by Edith Fowke. Reprinted by permission of The Canadian Publishers, McClelland and Stewart Limited, Toronto.

Who Stole My Chickens and My Hens?

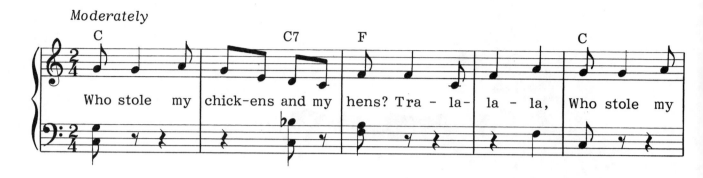

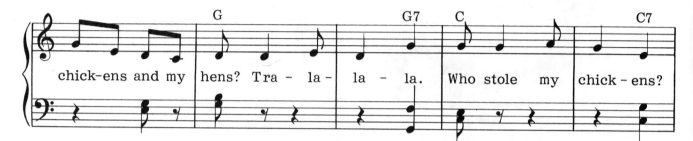

This song may be performed as a sort of "London Bridges" circle dance. "Farmer" and partner form an arch by joining hands and raising their arms up over their heads. Other children, in pairs, march through. On the last "la," the Farmer and partner drop hands and trap the "Thieves" (who then become the Farmer-couple for the next go-round).

From SALLY GO ROUND THE SUN by Edith Fowke. Reprinted by permission of The Canadian Publishers, McClelland and Stewart Limited, Toronto.

Rhythms

When I Take a Walk

Rhythmically

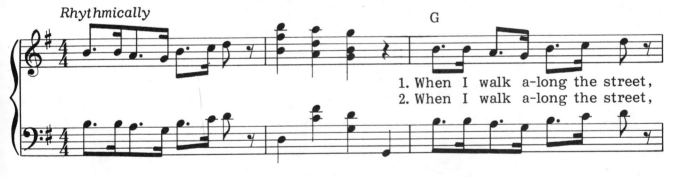

1. When I walk a-long the street,
2. When I walk a-long the street,

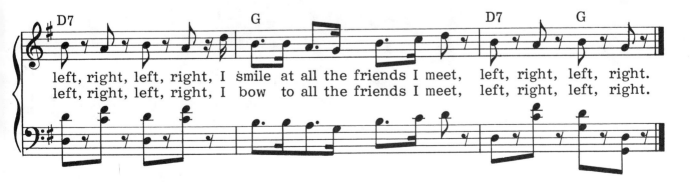

left, right, left, right, I smile at all the friends I meet, left, right, left, right.
left, right, left, right, I bow to all the friends I meet, left, right, left, right.

March of the Children

March of the Toys

Skip to My Lou

Lightly

Chorus

Lou, Lou, skip to my Lou, Lou, Lou, skip to my Lou,

Lou, Lou, skip to my Lou, Skip to my Lou, my dar - ling.

1. Lost my___ part - ner, what-'ll I___ do? Lost my___ part - ner, what-'ll I___ do?
2. I'll get an-oth-er one, pret-ti-er than you, I'll get an-oth-er one, pret-ti-er than you,

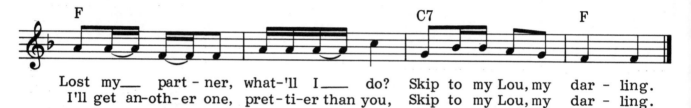

Lost my___ part - ner, what-'ll I___ do? Skip to my Lou, my dar - ling.
I'll get an-oth-er one, pret-ti-er than you, Skip to my Lou, my dar - ling.

3. Flies in the buttermilk, shoo, fly, shoo, etc.
4. Cows in the barnyard, moo, moo, moo, etc.
5. Train is a-coming, choo, choo, choo, etc.

Skipping: Old Joe Clark

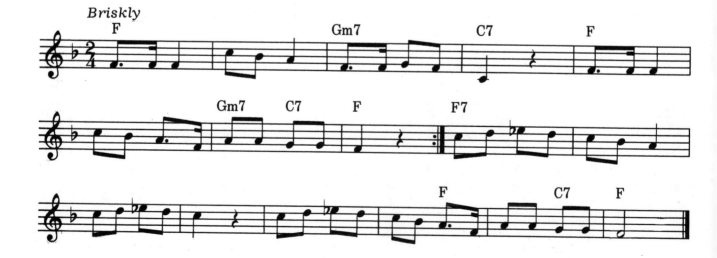

Briskly

Rig-a-Jig-Jig

As I was walk - ing down the street, Heigh-

o, heigh-o, heigh - o, heigh-o! A pret - ty girl I

chanced to meet, Heigh - o, heigh-o,____ heigh - o!

Chorus

Rig - a - jig-jig and a - way we go, a - way we go, a-

way we go, Rig - a - jig-jig and a - way we go, Heigh-

o, heigh-o,____ heigh - o! Heigh - o, heigh-o, heigh-

o, heigh-o, heigh - o, heigh-o, heigh - o, heigh-o!

Rig - a - jig - jig and a - way we go, Heigh - o, heigh-o,____ heigh-o!

Running

Galloping Horses

Briskly

Ride a-way on your hor - ses, your hor - ses, your hor - ses.

Ride a-way on your hor - ses.
1. Ride on, ride on.
2. Now whoa, whoa, whoa.

Gal-lop-ing, gal-lop-ing, gal-lop-ing, gal-lop-ing, gal-lop-ing, gal-lop-ing,

D.C. al Fine

gal-lop-ing, gal-lop-ing, on___ we___ go, oh!

The Little Gray Ponies

1. The lit-tle gray po-nies look out of the barn, And want to go out to play. The lit-tle gray po-nies jump o-ver the fence, And gal-lop and gal-lop a-way. And gal-lop and gal-lop a-way. And gal-lop and gal-lop a-way. 2. The

lit-tle gray po-nies jump o-ver the fence, And gal-lop and gal-lop a-way. The lit-tle gray po-nies come back to the barn; They're com-ing back home to stay! They're com-ing back home to stay! They're com-ing back home to stay!

Jumping and Flopping

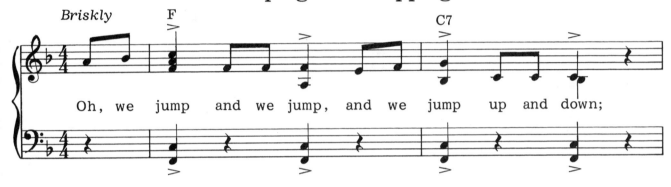

Oh, we jump and we jump, and we jump up and down;

Jump-ing, jump-ing, jump-ing up and down. Oh, we jump and we jump, and we

jump up and down; Jump, jump, jump, and then fall down.

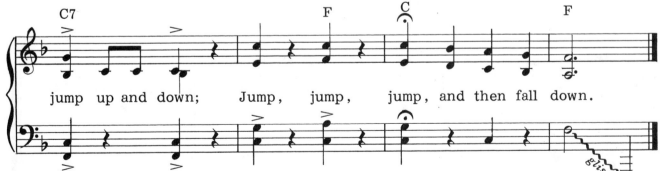

Other activities, such as hopping, sliding, stretching, stamp-
ing, kicking, etc., may be substituted .

Tip-Toe

Spinning Song

Russian Dance

Autumn
and
Halloween

Autumn's Here

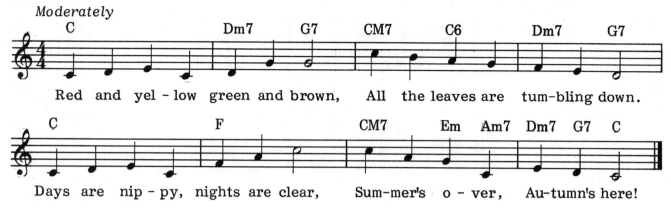

Red and yel-low green and brown, All the leaves are tum-bling down.
Days are nip-py, nights are clear, Sum-mer's o-ver, Au-tumn's here!

Autumn Leaves

Fall-ing, fall-ing, Au-tumn leaves are fall-ing. Fall-ing, fall-ing,

fall-ing on the ground. Whirl-ing, whirl-ing, Au-tumn leaves are

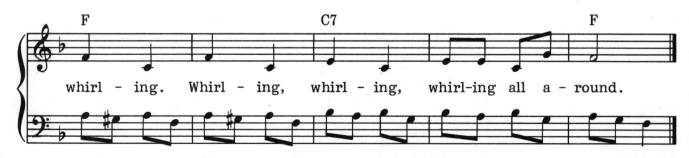

whirl-ing. Whirl-ing, whirl-ing, whirl-ing all a-round.

The Autumn Wind

Sadly — Dm ... A7

1. Oh, the au-tumn wind is a sor-ry wind, And it seems to cry ev-'ry day,
2. There are no more bright yel-low but-ter-flies That in days gone by it had known,

Dm ... Gm ... A7 ... Dm

For the au-tumn wind is a lone-some wind, When the birds and flow'rs go a-way.
So it sings a tune, such a lone-some tune, As it goes a-bout all a-lone.

"The Autumn Wind" by J. Lilian Vandevere. Used by permission of American Book Company.

Bobbing for Apples

Waltz

D ... G

1. Ap-ple, ap-ple, ap-ple,
2. Ap-ple, ap-ple, ap-ple,

A7 ... D ... A7 ... D

ap-ple, Float-ing in a pan; Bob-bing, bob-bing,
ap-ple, Hang-ing on a string; Bit-ing, bit-ing,

G ... A7 ... D

bob-bing, bob-bing, Catch one if you can.
bit-ing, bit-ing, Watch-ing ev-'ry swing.

From A SINGING SCHOOL: OUR FIRST MUSIC. Copyright © 1941 by C. C. Birchard & Co., copyright renewed © 1969. All rights reserved. Used by permission.

Christopher Columbo

Moderately

mf   < f   >   In

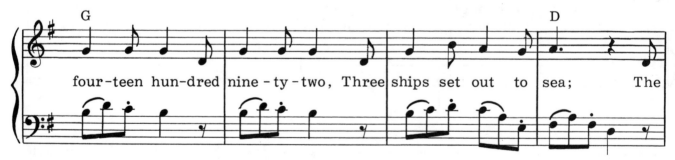

G   D

four-teen hun-dred nine-ty-two, Three ships set out to sea;   The

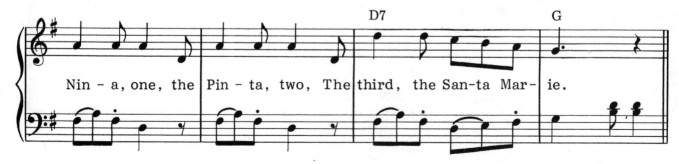

D7   G

Nin - a, one, the Pin - ta, two, The third, the San-ta Mar - ie.

He said the world was round-o, A-mer-i-ca he found-o, The

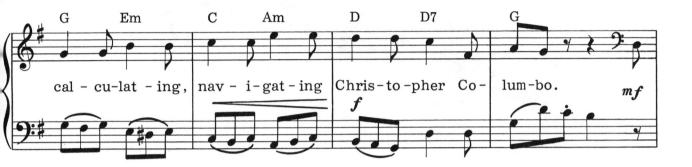

cal-cu-lat-ing, nav-i-gat-ing Chris-to-pher Co-lum-bo.

Christopher Columbus

Brightly

1. Chris-to-pher Co-lum-bus, sailed the o-cean blue; He
2. Sing a-bout Co-lum-bus, raise a heart-y cheer, And

brave-ly left the shore of Spain in four-teen nine-ty-two.
just be-cause he sailed so far and land-ed o-ver here.

Halloween's Here

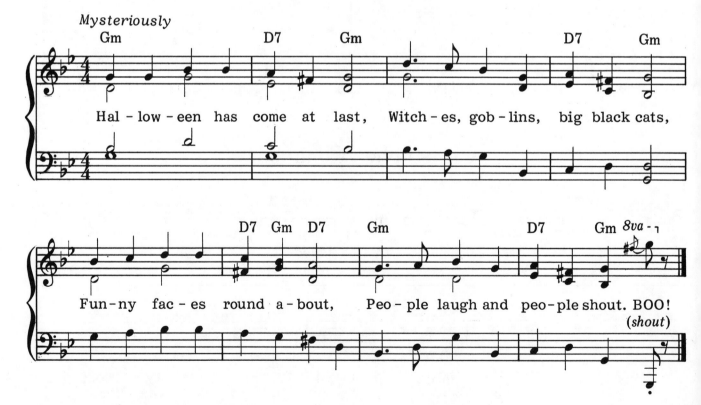

Mysteriously

Hal - low - een has come at last, Witch - es, gob - lins, big black cats,

Fun - ny fac - es round a - bout, Peo - ple laugh and peo - ple shout. BOO!
(shout)

The Witch Rides

Halloween Mask

55

Halloween

Slowly

mf

Eb   **Fm7**

1. It must be Hal - low - een, For when I hur-ried by,
2. He grinned with all___ his teeth From high up-on a shelf;

Bb7   *f*   **Eb**

A Jack - o'-lan-tern stared at me And winked his yel - low eye.___
I did-n't feel a - fraid, be-cause I'd cut him out my - self.___

"Halloween" by J. Lilian Vandevere. Used by permission of American Book Company.

Jack-O'-Lantern

Playfully

D   **Em**   **A7**   **D**

Jack - o'-lan - tern pump-kin head, He is a fear - ful sight!___

A   **E7**   **A7**

I am sure you'd be a - fraid to meet him in the night.___

D   **G**   **F#7**

He is by day a pump - kin, But just you wait till night,___

Bm   **Em7**   **D**   **A7**   **D**

When out of eyes and nose and mouth, There shines a yel - low light!___

Have You Seen the Ghost of John?

Spookily

① Have you seen the ghost of John?

② Long white bones and the rest all gone,

③ Ooh, ooh,

④ Would-n't it be chil-ly with no skin on?

From THE FIRESIDE BOOK OF CHILDREN'S SONGS by Marie Winn and Allan Miller. Copyright © 1966 by Marie Winn and Allan Miller. Reprinted by permission of Simon & Schuster, a Division of Gulf & Western Corporation.

Halloween Night

Gaily

1. Let's have a party on Hal - low - een night,
2. John - ny will come in some fun - ny old clothes,

Gob - lins and witch - es to give us a fright!
Flop - py old hat and a long point - ed nose.

Af - ter some games we will all have a treat,
Bil - ly's a cow - boy and Bet - ty's a clown,

Ap - ples and cook - ies and can - dy to eat;
Ma - ry's a ghost, with a sheet for a gown;

Oh, what a par - ty on Hal - low - een night!
Ev - 'ry - one fro - lics in Hal - low - een clothes!

From TOGETHER WE SING by Irving Wolfe and Margaret Fullerton. Copyright © 1953 by Margaret Fullerton. Used by permission of Follett Publishing Company.

Indians and Thanksgiving

Indian Dance

Dakota

Prayer for Rain

In My Birch Canoe

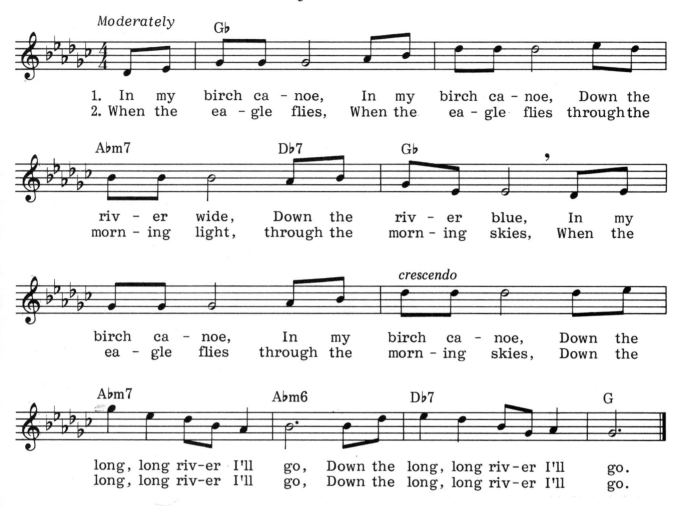

1. In my birch ca - noe, In my birch ca - noe, Down the
2. When the ea - gle flies, When the ea - gle flies through the

riv - er wide, Down the riv - er blue, In my
morn - ing light, through the morn - ing skies, When the

birch ca - noe, In my birch ca - noe, Down the
ea - gle flies through the morn - ing skies, Down the

long, long riv-er I'll go, Down the long, long riv-er I'll go.
long, long riv-er I'll go, Down the long, long riv-er I'll go.

3. When the running deer, when the running deer,
   Through the forest green seeks the water clear,
   Down the long, long river I'll go,
   Down the long, long river I'll go.

Canoe Song

Steadily   Round

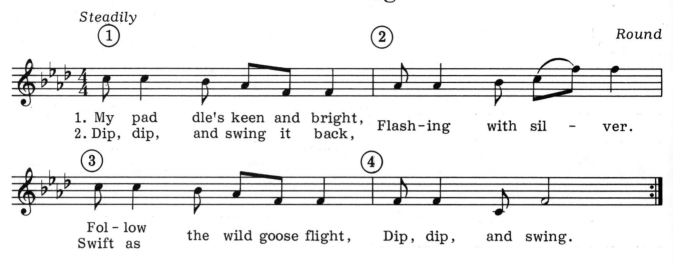

1. My paddle's keen and bright, Flash-ing with sil - ver.
2. Dip, dip, and swing it back, Flash-ing with sil - ver.

Fol - low the wild goose flight, Dip, dip, and swing.
Swift as the wild goose flight, Dip, dip, and swing.

Follow the Leader

Ojibway

Steadily

Repeat ad lib. 1. Fol - low, fol - low, fol - low
Mu - je mu - ke - sin au-

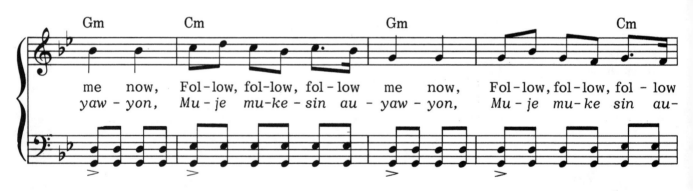

me now, Fol-low, fol-low, fol-low me now, Fol-low, fol-low, fol - low
yaw - yon, Mu je mu-ke - sin au - yaw - yon, Mu je mu-ke sin au-

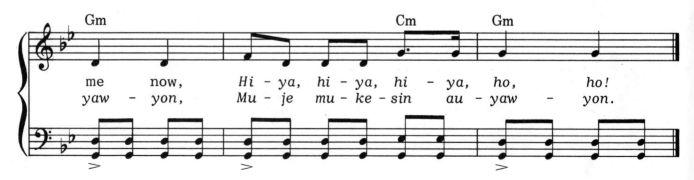

me now, Hi - ya, hi - ya, hi - ya, ho, ho!
yaw - yon, Mu - je mu - ke - sin au - yaw - yon.

Hi-Yo-Witzi (*Morning Song*)

Hi - yo___ hi-yo-wit-zi nai - yo.

Hi - yo___ hi - yo - wit - zi nai - yo.___

Hi - yo nai - yo hi!___

Melody and words by Chief White Eagle from THE UNIVERSAL SONGSTER, simplified by Florence Hudson Botsford. Copyright © 1936 by G. Schirmer, Inc. Used by permission.

Blue Corn Grinding Song

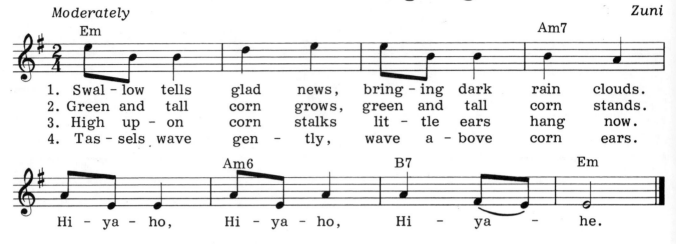

Moderately   *Zuni*

1. Swal – low tells glad news, bring – ing dark rain clouds.
2. Green and tall corn grows, green and tall corn stands.
3. High up – on corn stalks lit – tle ears hang now.
4. Tas – sels wave gen – tly, wave a – bove corn ears.

Hi – ya – ho, Hi – ya – ho, Hi – ya – he.

My Owlet

Kiowa

Rhythmically

Ow – let, my ow – let is sleep – ing.

pp

Wee stars are twink – ling in the sky.
Moth – er is sing – ing lul – la – by.

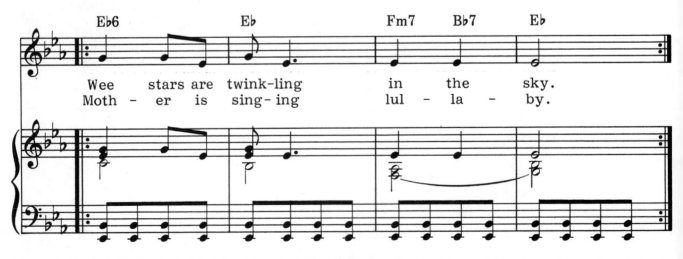

Proud Turkeys

Moderately

Tur-keys stretch their necks and strut, Spread their feath-ers wide.

All they say is "Gob-ble, gob-ble, gob ble," As they wob-ble from side to side.

The Turkey

Polish Folk Tune

This old road is hard and bump-y, Our new tur-key's wild and jump-y.
De-bre tsen-be kay-ne men-ni, Puy-kah-kah-kasht kay-ne ven-ni,

Driv-er! Driv-er! Not so jerk-y! Or you'll make us lose our tur-key.
Vee-dyaz ko-cheesh yu-kash, a kash, Kee-eh-shik a puy-kah-kah-kash.

The Turkeys Run Away

1. With a wob-ble, wob-ble, wob-ble, and a gob-ble, gob-ble, gob-ble,
2. When they see the farm-er com-ing, all the tur-keys start a-run-ning,

All the tur-keys spread their feath-ers on Thanks-giv-ing Day.
And they say, "You can-not catch us on Thanks-giv-ing Day!"

From THIS IS MUSIC BOOK I by William R. Sur, Adeline McCall, William R. Fisher, and Mary R. Tolbert. Copyright © 1967 by Allyn & Bacon, Inc. Used by permission.

Gobble, Gobble

A tur-key sat on a back-yard fence and he sang this sad, sad tune—Thanks-giving day is com-ing, gob-ble, gob-ble, gob-ble, gob-ble, And I know I'll be eat-en soon._____ Gob-ble, gob-ble, gob-ble, gob-ble, gob-ble, gob-ble, gob-ble. How I'd like to run a-way._____ Gob-ble, gob-ble, gob-ble, gob-ble, gob-ble, gob-ble, gob-ble, I don't like Thanks-giv-ing day.

Over the River

Brightly

1. O-ver the riv-er, and through the wood, To grand-fa-ther's house we go;___ The
2. O-ver the riv-er, and through the wood-When grand-mo-ther sees us come,___ She

horse knows the way to car-ry the sleigh through the white and drift-ed snow.___
will say,"Oh, dear, the chil-dren are here, bring a pie for ever-y one."___

O-ver the riv-er, and through the wood, To grand-fa-ther's house a-way!___ We
O-ver the riv-er, and through the wood-Now grand-mo-ther's cap I spy!___ Hur-

would not stop for doll or top, for 'tis Thanks-giv-ing Day.___
rah for the fun! Is the pud-ding done? Hur-rah for the pump-kin - pie!___

Turkey in the Straw

Lively

1. As I was a-rid-in' down the road, With a
2. Went out to milk and I did-n't know how, I

tired team and a hea-vy load, I cracked my whip and the
milked the goat in-stead of the cow. A mon-key sit-tin' on a

lead-er sprung; I says day-day to the wa-gon tongue.
pile of straw A-wink-in' at his moth-er-in-law.

Chorus

Tur-key in the straw, *(whistle)* tur-key in the hay,

(whistle) Roll 'em up and twist 'em up a high tuck-a-haw, And

hit 'em up a tune called Tur-key in the Straw.

3. Met Mr. Catfish comin' down stream,
   Says Mr. Catfish, "What do you mean?"
   Caught Mr. Catfish by the snout
   And turned Mr. Catfish wrong side out.
   Chorus

4. Came to the river and I couldn't get across,
   Paid five dollars for an old blind hoss,
   Wouldn't go ahead, nor he wouldn't stand still,
   So he went up and down like an old saw mill.
   Chorus

5. As I came down the new cut road,
   Met Mr. Bullfrog, met Miss Toad,
   And every time Miss Toad would sing
   Ole Bullfrog cut a pigeon wing.
   Chorus

6. Oh, I jumped in the seat, and I gave a little shout,
   The horses run away, broke the wagon all about,
   Sugar in the gourd and honey in the horn,
   I never was so happy since the hour I was born.
   Chorus

Lyrics and Melody of "Turkey in the Straw" from THE HOLIDAY SONGBOOK by Robert Quackenbush. Copyright © 1977 by Robert Quackenbush. Reprinted by permission of Lothrop, Lee & Shepard (A Division of William Morrow & Company).

Thanksgiving Hymn

From SINGING HOLIDAYS by Oscar Brand. Copyright © 1957 by Oscar Brand. Published by Alfred A. Knopf.

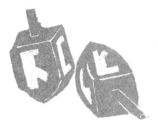

Hanukkah
and
Christmas

My Dreydle

Clearly

I have a lit-tle drey-dle, A pret-ty lit-tle top; A-

round and round it's spin-ning, I'll nev-er let it stop! Oh,

drey-dle, drey-dle, drey-dle, Oh, lit-tle top that spins! The

chil-dren all are hap-py When Ha-nuk-kah be-gins.

Shalom Chaverim

Come Light the Menorah

hora: a circle dance   *levivot:* dumplings

From THE GATEWAY TO JEWISH SONG by Judith K. Eisenstein. Reprinted by permission of Behrman House, Inc. and the author.

Hora

There are four counts to each measure and a step for each count. Begin with feet together and head lowered. On count 1, step to the side with the left foot. On count 2, tap the right foot behind the left. On count 3, raise head, hop on left foot and kick right foot forward. On count 4, hop on right foot and kick left foot forward. The dance may be done in one large circle or in two smaller circles, one inside the other. For variation, have the inner circle begin on the right foot.

Christmas Is Coming

Lively

1. Christ - mas is com - ing, The goose is get - ting fat!

Please to put a pen - ny in the old man's hat!

Please to put a pen - ny in the old man's hat!

By permission of Barthold Fles, Literary Agent.

2. If you have no penny,
   A ha' penny will do,
   If you have no ha' penny,
   A farthing will do,
   If you have no farthing,
   Then God bless you!

We're Coming To Greet You

Puerto Rican

Brightly

1. We're com - ing to greet you, this hol - i - day gay, We're

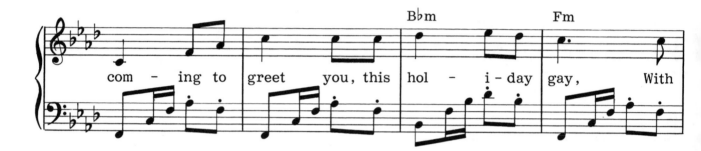

com - ing to greet you, this hol - i - day gay, With

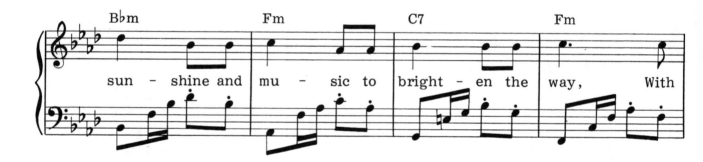

sun - shine and mu - sic to bright - en the way, With

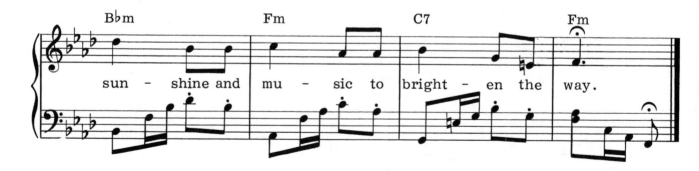

sun - shine and mu - sic to bright - en the way.

2. So welcome us, please, with some holiday cheer,
So welcome us, please, with some holiday cheer,
'Tis Christmas, the happiest time of the year,
'Tis Christmas, the happiest time of the year.

Deck the Halls

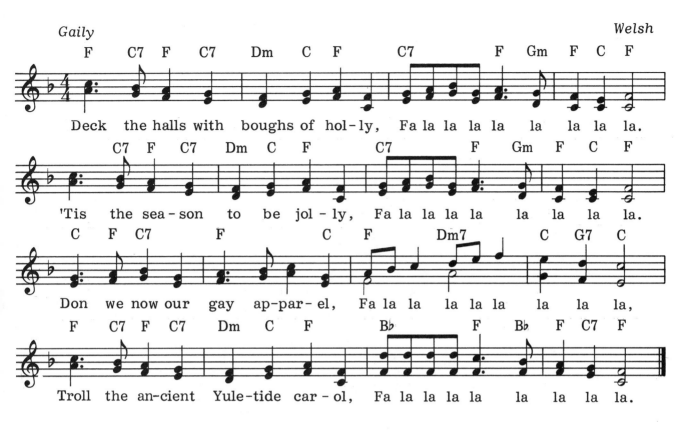

Gaily
Welsh

Deck the halls with boughs of hol-ly, Fa la la la la la la la la.

'Tis the sea-son to be jol-ly, Fa la la la la la la la la.

Don we now our gay ap-par-el, Fa la la la la la la la la,

Troll the an-cient Yule-tide car-ol, Fa la la la la la la la la.

Jingle Bells

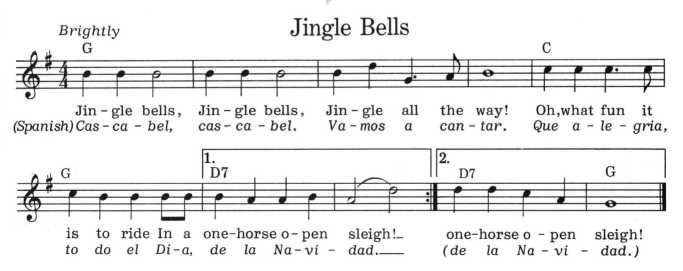

Brightly

Jin - gle bells, Jin - gle bells, Jin - gle all the way! Oh, what fun it
(Spanish) Cas - ca - bel, cas - ca - bel. Va - mos a can - tar. Que a - le - gria,

is to ride In a one-horse o - pen sleigh!_ one-horse o - pen sleigh!
to do el Di - a, de la Na - vi - dad.___ (de la Na - vi - dad.)

Good King Wenceslas

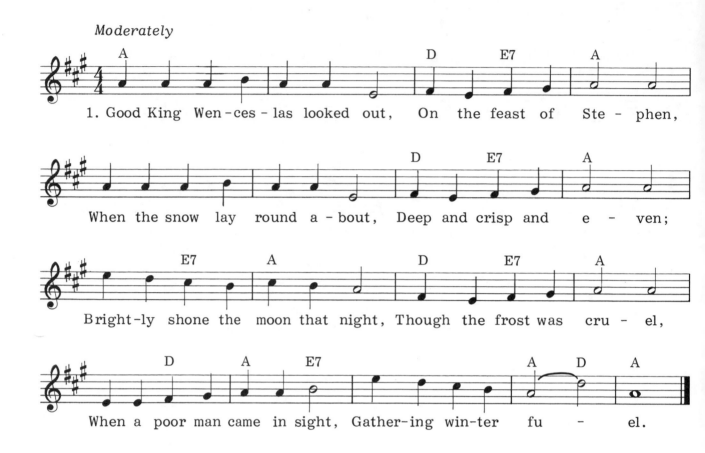

Moderately

1. Good King Wen-ces-las looked out, On the feast of Ste - phen,
When the snow lay round a - bout, Deep and crisp and e - ven;
Bright-ly shone the moon that night, Though the frost was cru - el,
When a poor man came in sight, Gather-ing win-ter fu - el.

2. "Hither, page, and stand by me,
   If thou know'st it, telling,
   Yonder peasant, who is he?
   Where and what his dwelling?"
   "Sir, he lives a good league hence,
   Underneath the mountain,
   Right against the forest fence,
   By St. Agnes' fountain."

3. "Bring me meat and bring me wine,
   Bring me pine-logs hither:
   Thou and I will see him dine,
   When we bear them thither."
   Page and monarch forth they went,
   Forth they went together;
   Through the rude wind's wild lament
   And the bitter weather.

4. "Sire, the night is darker now,
   And the wind blows stronger;
   Fails my heart, I know not how,
   I can go no longer."
   "Mark my foot steps, good my page;
   Tread thou in them boldly:
   Thou shalt find the winter's rage
   Freeze thy blood less coldly."

5. In his master's steps he trod,
   Where the snow lay dinted;
   Heat was in the very sod
   Which the saint had printed.
   Therefore, Christian men, be sure,
   Wealth or rank possessing,
   Ye who will now bless the poor,
   Shall your selves find blessing.

O Christmas Tree

German

Moderately

1. O Tan-nen-baum, O Tan-nen-baum, Wie treu sind dei - ne Blät - ter!
1. O Christ-mas tree, O Christ-mas tree, With faith-ful leaves un-chang-ing;

O Tan-nen-baum, O Tan-nen-baum, Wie treu sind dei - ne Blät - ter!
O Christ-mas tree, O Christ-mas tree, With faith-ful leaves un - chang-ing;

Du grünst nich nur zur Som-mers-zeit, Nein, auch im Win - ter, wen-nes schneit
Not on - ly green in sum-mer's heat, But al - so win - ter's snow and sleet,

O Tan-nen-baum, O Tan-nen-baum, Wie treu sind dei - ne Blät - ter!
O Christ-mas tree, O Christ-mas tree, With faith-ful leaves un - chang-ing.

2. O Tannenbaum, O Tannenbaum,
Du kannst mir sehr gefallen. (repeat)
Wie oft hat nicht zur Weihnachtszeit
Ein Baum von dir mich hoch erfreut!
O Tannenbaum, O Tannenbaum,
Du kannst mir sehr gefallen.

2. O Christmas tree, O Christmas tree,
Of all the trees most lovely, (repeat)
Each year, you bring to me delight
Gleaming in the Christmas light.
O Christmas tree, O Christmas tree,
Of all the trees most lovely.

Christmas Eve Canon

The parents should sing the first line alone and then keep on repeating it so long as the children keep up their two-part round.

By permission of Barthold Fles, Literary Agent.

A Cradle Carol

Russian Folk Tune

1. Long a-go and far a-way, far a-way,
2. Ba-by Je-sus woke and smiled, woke and smiled,

Fast a-sleep a ba-by lay, ba-by lay, O-ver-head a song filled the
Wise men came to see the child, see the child, Cra-dled in the hay He was

qui-et night, O-ver-head a star gave a love-ly light.
ver-y small, Still He was a king, and the Lord of all.

We Wish You a Merry Christmas

We wish you a Mer-ry Christ-mas. We wish you a Mer-ry Christ-mas.

We wish you a Mer-ry Christ-mas, and a Hap-py New Year!

The First Nowell

The_ first_ Now - ell, the_ an gel did say,

Was to cer - tain poor shep-herds in fields as they lay;

In_ fields_ where_ they lay_ keep - ing their sheep,

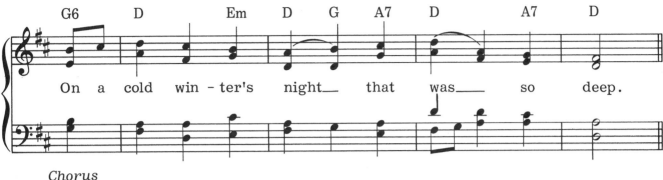

On a cold win-ter's night that was__ so deep.

Chorus

Now - ell,__ Now - ell, Now - ell, Now - ell,

Born is the King__ of Is - ra - el.

Cradle Song from Haiti

2. Jesu! Wise men came from far,
   Jesu! Guided by the star;
   Humbly Thee they sought,
   Gold and incense sweet, rich gifts
   From the East to Thee they brought.
   Jesu! Thou dear Babe divine.

3. Jesu! Come we now to Thee,
   Jesu! Lowly bend the knee:
   We Thy grace implore;
   Lord, we too, with childlike hearts,
   At the manger Thee adore.
   Jesu! Thou dear Babe divine.

English text by Helen A. Dickinson. Arranged by Clarence Dickinson. Published as "Jesu! Thou Dear Babe Divine." Copyright 1915 by the H. W. Gray Company (A Division of Belwin-Mills Publishing Corp.) Copyright renewed 1943. Used by permission.

The Three Kings

Moderately

1. We three kings of O-ri-ent are; Bear-ing gifts, we trav-el a-far Field and foun-tain, moor and moun-tain, Fol-low-ing yon-der star.

Chorus

O——— star of won-der, star of night, Star with roy-al beau-ty bright, West-ward lead-ing still pro-ceed-ing, Guide us to Thy per-fect light.

Fum, fum, fum!

Spanish

Rhythmically

1. On De-cem-ber twen-ty-five, sing foom, foom, foom!
1. ¡Vein - ti -cin - co de di -ciem-bre, fum, fum, fum!

On De-cem-ber twen-ty-five, sing foom, foom, foom! He is
¡Vein - ti -cin - co de di -ciem-bre, fum, fum, fum! Na-ci-

born for love of us, The lit-tle God, the ba-by God: Of the
do ha por nues-tro a mor, el Ni-ño Dios, el Ni-ño Dios; hoy de

mp

lightly

Vir-gin born a-live this cold De-cem-ber twen-ty-five, Sing foom, foom, foom!
la vir-gen Ma-rí-a en es-ta no-che tan fri-a, ¡Fum, fum, fum!

sf   *mp*   *p*

2. Little birds from out the woods,
   Sing foom, foom, foom!
   Little birds from out the woods,
   Sing foom, foom, foom!
   Leave the little ones at home,
   Abandon them, abandon them;
   Form a cozy nest to please us
   For the little baby Jesus,
   Foom, foom, foom!

3. Little stars up in the sky,
   Sing foom, foom, foom!
   Little stars up in the sky,
   Sing foom, foom, foom!
   You may look at Jesus crying
   But yourselves must not be crying;
   Make the dark night glitter lightly,
   Make it twinkle purely, brightly,
   Foom, foom, foom!

2. *¡Pajaritos de los bosques,*
   fum, fum, fum!
   ¡Pajaritos de los bosques,
   fum, fum, fum!
   vuestros hijos de coral
   abandonad, abandonad,
   y formad un muelle nido
   a Jesús recién nacido,
   Fum, fum, fum!

3. *¡Estrellitas de los cielos,*
   fum, fum, fum!
   ¡Estrellitas de los cielos,
   fum, fum, fum!
   que a Jesús miráis llorar
   y no lloráis, y no lloráis,
   alumbrad la noche oscura
   con vuestra luz clara y pura,
   ¡Fum, fum, fum!

By permission of Barthold Fles, Literary Agent.

Patapan

French Folk Tune

Brightly

Wil - lie take your lit - tle drum, With his flute let Rob - in come, Play as loud - ly as you can; Tu - re - lu - re - lu, pat - a - pat - a - pan. Make a mu - sic bright and gay, Play a - way, It is Christ - mas Day.____

The Twelve Days of Christmas

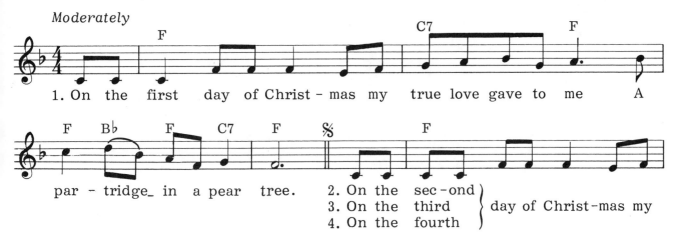

Moderately

1. On the first day of Christ-mas my true love gave to me A

par-tridge in a pear tree.
2. On the sec-ond ⎱
3. On the third ⎰ day of Christ-mas my
4. On the fourth ⎰

New Year's Song

Clearly

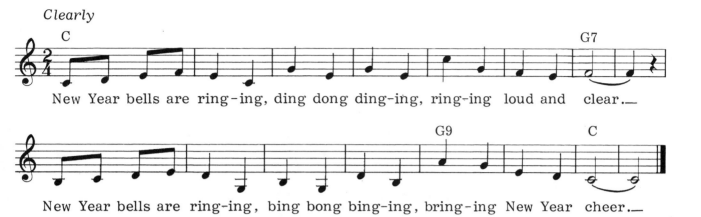

New Year bells are ring-ing, ding dong ding-ing, ring-ing loud and clear.—

New Year bells are ring-ing, bing bong bing-ing, bring-ing New Year cheer.—

Winter

Jack Frost

Crisply

The tem-p'ra-ture is freez-ing. It's less than thir-ty - two. 'Cause look who's on my win - dow. It's Jack___ Frost, that's who!

The North Wind Doth Blow

Lightly

The north wind doth blow,— We soon shall have snow, And what will poor rob-in do then, poor thing? He'll sit in the barn— to keep him-self warm, And hide his head un-der his wing, poor thing.

Reprinted by permission of Inez B. McClintock, the author.

Whirling Snowflakes

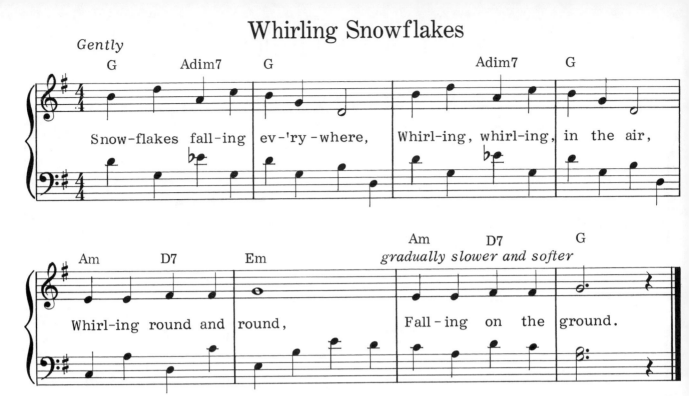

Gently

Snow-flakes fall-ing ev-'ry-where, Whirl-ing, whirl-ing, in the air,

Whirl-ing round and round, Fall-ing on the ground.

gradually slower and softer

From THIS IS MUSIC FOR KINDERGARTEN AND NURSERY SCHOOL by Adeline McCall. Copyright © 1965 by Allyn & Bacon, Inc. Used by Permission.

Fun in the Snow

Playfully

1. It's fun to play in the
2. It's fun to play in the

snow._____ Bun-dled warm as toast._____
snow._____ Take your sled and coast._____

From THIS IS MUSIC FOR KINDERGARTEN AND NURSERY SCHOOL by Adeline McCall. Copyright © 1965 by Allyn & Bacon, Inc. Used by permission.

Snow Balls

Moderately

1. The snow is soft for the snow ball fight.} Roll it
2. We'll build a fort where we hide from sight.} Roll it

round and read-y to throw. throw. Roll it

round and hard, roll it round and hard, Roll it round and read-y to throw.

Making a Snow Man

Roll it, roll it, get a pile of snow, Roll-ing, roll-ing, roll-ing, roll-ing,

roll-ing, here we go, Pat it, pat it, face it to the south.

Now my lit - tle snow man's done, eyes and nose and mouth.

(f)

Mitten Song

Briskly

1. "Thumbs in the thumb – place, Fin – gers all to – geth – er!"
2. When it is cold, It does – n't mat – ter wheth – er
3. This is the song, We sing in mit – ten weath – er:

This is the song, We sing in mit – ten weath – er.
Mit – tens are wool, Or made of fin – est leath – er.
"Thumbs in the thumb – place, Fin – gers all to – geth – er!"

Text of "The Mitten Song" from A POCKETFUL OF POEMS by Marie Louise Allen. Text copyright © 1957 by Marie Allen Howarth. Reprinted by permission of Harper and Row, Publishers, Inc.

Music from OUR SINGING WORLD: THE FIRST GRADE BOOK. Copyright © 1959 by Ginn & Co.

Zippers

Moderately

1. Three lit – tle zip – pers on my snow suit,
2. I work the zip – pers on my snow suit,

Fas – ten up as snug as snug can be, It's a ver – y eas – y thing, as
Zip – pers real – ly do save time for me. I can fas – ten them my – self, with

you can see, Just zip!__ zip!__ zip!__
one, two, three, Just zip!__ zip!__ zip!__

Ice Skating

Carefully

Ice skat-ing is nice skat-ing, But here's some ad-vice a-bout

ice skat-ing: Nev - er skate where the ice is thin,

Thin ice will crack and you'll fall right in, And come up with i-ci-cles

un-der your chin, If you skate where the ice is thin.____

Winter Holidays

George Washington

1. Man - y, man - y years a go when our coun - try was still young,__ There
2. He be - came a gen - er - al, our__ arm - ies to com - mand,__ Then

lived a man so strong and brave, his name was Wash - ing - ton.__
he was made the Pres - i - dent, the first one in the land.__

On his birth - day let's sing in cel - e - bra - tion;__

We re - mem - ber Wash - ing - ton, the fa - ther of our na - tion.__

Duke of York

Spiritedly

1. Oh, the no-ble Duke of York,— He had ten thou-sand men,— He
2. Oh, a hunt-ing we will go,— A-hunt-ing we will go,— We'll

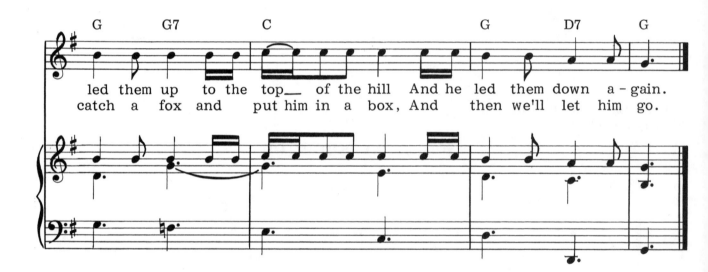

led them up to the top— of the hill And he led them down a-gain.
catch a fox and put him in a box, And then we'll let him go.

A-Hunting We Will Go

Have children form a circle and join hands. One child, chosen to be the Fox, stands outside the circle.

On the first time through the verse, children circle to the left while they sing the first two lines, and the Fox skips to the right outside the circle. Children circle to the right while singing the next two lines, and the Fox skips to the left outside the circle.

On the second time through the verse, the two children nearest the Fox raise their arms (creating an arch) and force the Fox into the circle by bringing the arch down on the other side of him. Children sing and slowly close ranks, holding hands and walking toward the center of the circle. They trap the Fox within a tight circle and bounce him around until the word "go," when they raise their arms and let him free. He chooses another child to be the next Fox and the game is repeated.

Yankee Doodle

Jauntily

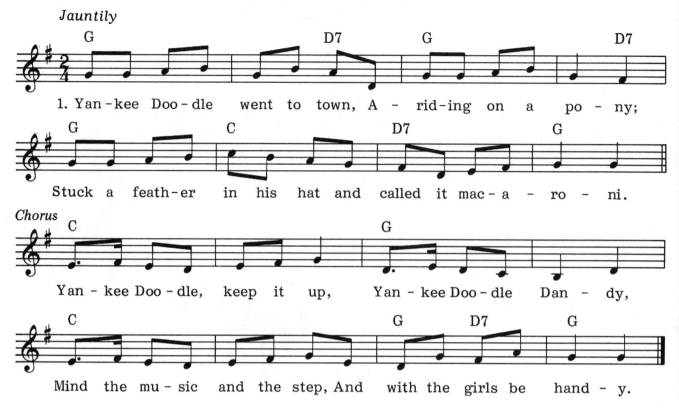

1. Yan-kee Doo-dle went to town, A-rid-ing on a po-ny;

Stuck a feath-er in his hat and called it mac-a-ro-ni.

Chorus

Yan-kee Doo-dle, keep it up, Yan-kee Doo-dle Dan-dy,

Mind the mu-sic and the step, And with the girls be hand-y.

2. There was Captain Washington upon a
   slapping stallion. A-giving orders to his men;
   I guess there were a million.
   Chorus

My Hat It Has Three Corners

Moderately

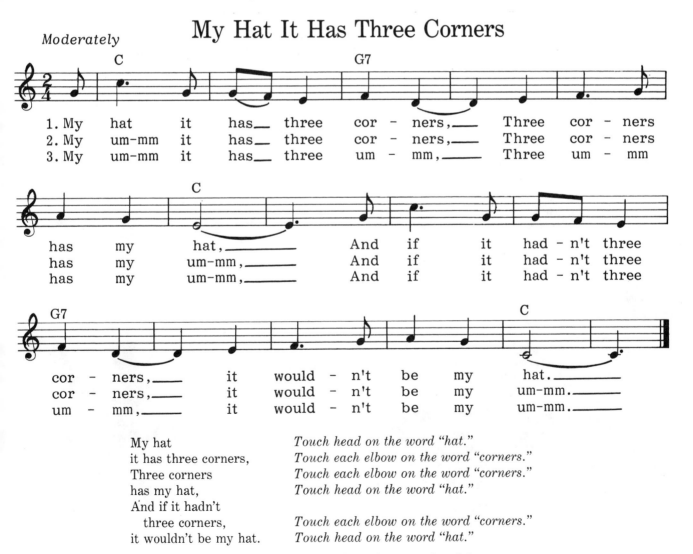

1. My hat it has__ three cor - ners,__ Three cor - ners
2. My um-mm it has__ three cor - ners,__ Three cor - ners
3. My um-mm it has__ three um - mm,__ Three um - mm

has my hat,_____ And if it had - n't three
has my um-mm,_____ And if it had - n't three
has my um-mm,_____ And if it had - n't three

cor - ners,____ it would - n't be my hat.
cor - ners,____ it would - n't be my um-mm.
um - mm,____ it would - n't be my um-mm.

My hat	*Touch head on the word "hat."*
it has three corners,	*Touch each elbow on the word "corners."*
Three corners	*Touch each elbow on the word "corners."*
has my hat,	*Touch head on the word "hat."*
And if it hadn't	
three corners,	*Touch each elbow on the word "corners."*
it wouldn't be my hat.	*Touch head on the word "hat."*

Continue the action through verses 2 and 3.

Old Abe Lincoln

Rhythmically

1. Old Abe Lin-coln, he came out of the wil-der-ness,
2. Old Abe Lin-coln, he moved in-to the White House,

Out of the wil-der-ness, out of the wil-der-ness;
In-to the White House, in-to the White House;

Old Abe Lin-coln, he came out of the wil-der-ness,
Old Abe Lin-coln, he moved in-to the White House,

Down in Il-li-nois.
Man-y long years a-go.

The Battle Hymn of the Republic

Majestically

Mine eyes have seen the glo-ry of the com-ing of the Lord; He is
tram-pling out the vin-tage where the grapes of wrath are stored; He hath
loosed the fate-ful light-ning of his ter-ri-ble swift sword; His
truth is march-ing on.
Glo-ry! glo-ry, hal-le-lu - jah! Glo-ry! glo-ry, hal-le-lu - jah!
Glo-ry! glo-ry, hal-le-lu - jah! His truth is march-ing on.

We Shall Overcome

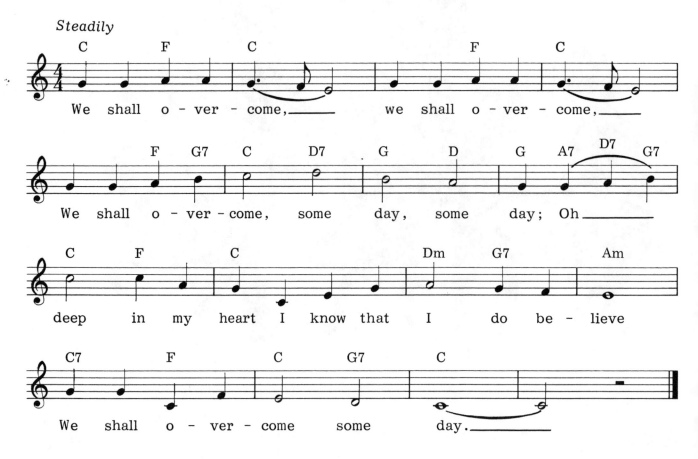

Steadily

We shall o - ver - come,_____ we shall o - ver - come,_____

We shall o - ver - come, some day, some day; Oh_____

deep in my heart I know that I do be - lieve

We shall o - ver - come some day._____

New words and musical arrangement by Zilphia Horton, Frank Hamilton, Guy Carawar & Pete Seeger. TRO— © Copyright 1960 & 1963 LUDLOW MUSIC, INC., New York, N.Y. Used by permission.

Valentine Song

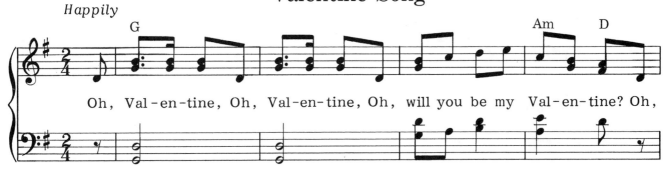

Happily

G ... Am ... D

Oh, Val-en-tine, Oh, Val-en-tine, Oh, will you be my Val-en-tine? Oh,

D7 ... G ... D7 ... G

Val-en-tine, Oh, Val-en-tine, Oh, will you be my Val-en-tine?

Clementine

Moderately

1. In a cav-ern, in a can-yon, Ex-ca-va-ting for a mine, Lived a
2. Light she was and like a fair-y, And her shoes were num-ber nine, Her-ring

min-er for-ty nin-er, And his daugh-ter Cle-men-tine.}
box-es with-out top-ses, San-dals were for Cle-men-tine.}

Chorus

Oh my dar-ling, oh my dar-ling, oh my dar-ling, Cle-men-tine! Thou art

lost and gone for ev-er, dread-ful sor-ry, Cle-men-tine.

3. Drove her ducklings to the water,
   Every morning just at nine,
   Hit her foot against a splinter,
   Fell into the foaming brine.
   Chorus

4. Saw her lips above the water,
   Blowing bubbles mighty fine,
   But alas! I was no swimmer,
   So I lost my Clementine.
   Chorus

5. Listen Boy Scouts, heed the warning
   Of this tragic tale of mine:
   Artificial respiration
   Could have saved my Clementine.
   Chorus

6. How I missed her, how I missed her,
   How I missed my Clementine!
   Then I kissed her little sister
   And forgot my Clementine.
   Chorus

If All of the Raindrops

Liltingly

If all____ the rain-drops were lem-on drops and gum-drops,

oh what a rain it would be. I'd stand out-side with my mouth o-pen wide.

That's__ the weath-er for me. _____ I would-n't care if the

sun would nev-er shine. I'd keep on wish-ing for rain-drops all the time.

"If All of the Raindrops Were Lemon Drops and Gumdrops," from CAMP SONGS, sung by Pete Seeger on Scholastic/Folkways Record #7028.

Raindrops

Cheerfully

When we play we're rain - drops danc - ing on the street,

Pit - ter pat - ter, pit - ter pat - ter, with our lit - tle feet.

Swish - y, swash - y, swish - y, swash - y. Rain be - tween our feet.

When we play we're rain - drops, danc - ing on the street.

From THE SUNFLOWER SONGBOOK by June Norton. Copyright © 1935, 1956, 1963 by June Mary Norton and Charlotte Byj. Published by John Day. Used by permission of Thomas Y. Crowell.

Nesting Time

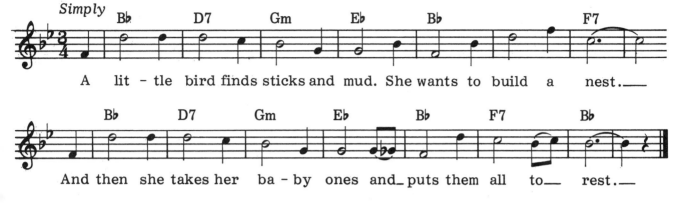

A lit-tle bird finds sticks and mud. She wants to build a nest.___

And then she takes her ba-by ones and_ puts them all to_ rest.___

A Little Bird

1. A lit-tle bird in an ap-ple tree, was sing-ing this pret-ty
2. I tried and tried to___ climb that tree, but I kept___ fall-ing

song to me, "Oh! climb up here and___ you will see a
on my knee. The bir-die said, "Lift your wings like me," I

but-ter-fly chas-ing a bum-ble bee." did and I flew up in the ap-ple tree.

Zip-A-Dee-Doo-Dah

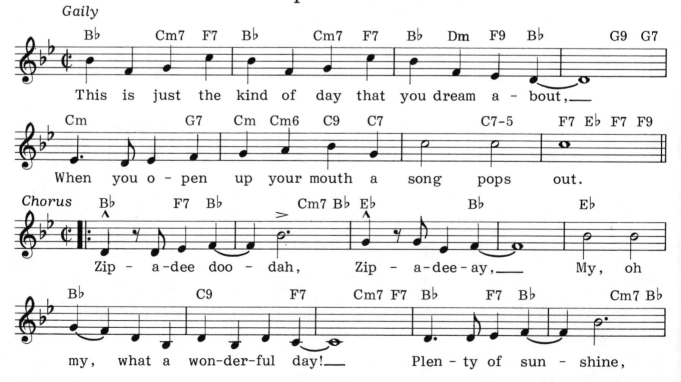

Gaily

Bb | Cm7 F7 Bb | Cm7 F7 Bb | Dm F9 Bb | G9 G7

This is just the kind of day that you dream a - bout,___

Cm | G7 Cm Cm6 C9 C7 | | C7-5 | F7 Eb F7 F9

When you o - pen up your mouth a song pops out.

Chorus

Bb | F7 Bb | Cm7 Bb Eb | Bb | Eb

Zip - a-dee doo - dah, Zip - a-dee-ay,___ My, oh

Bb | C9 | F7 | Cm7 F7 Bb | F7 Bb | Cm7 Bb

my, what a won-der-ful day!___ Plen - ty of sun - shine,

Eb		Bb		Eb		Bb	Gm Cm7	F9 Bb

head-in' my way,___ Zip - a-dee doo - dah, Zip - a-dee - ay!___

Eb | | F7 | F9 | | F7 | C#dim Bb | | Gm7

___ Mis-ter Blue-bird on my shoul - der,___ It's the

C7 | C9 | C7 | | F Tacet

truth, it's "act-ch'll," Ev-'ry-thing is "sa - tis fact-ch'll."

Bb | | F7 .Bb | | Cm Bb Eb | | Bb

Zip - a-dee doo - dah, Zip - a-dee - ay!___

Eb | | Bb | Gm | C7 | F7 Bb |1 Edim F7 |2.

Won - der-ful feel - ing, Won - der-ful day.___

Mister Wind

Playfully

Oh! Mis - ter Wind with a whirl and a jig came blow-ing up the street.

He blew off my hat and he blew off my coat and he blew me off my feet.

Oh! Mis - ter Wind, you're much too strong for a lit - tle boy like me;

You blew off my hat, you blew off my coat, and blew me off my feet.

Get up, lit - tle boy, Now please don't cry, I'll help you all I can.

I'll fly your kite and I'll sail your boat, way off to make-be-lieve land.

Who Has Seen the Wind?

Smoothly

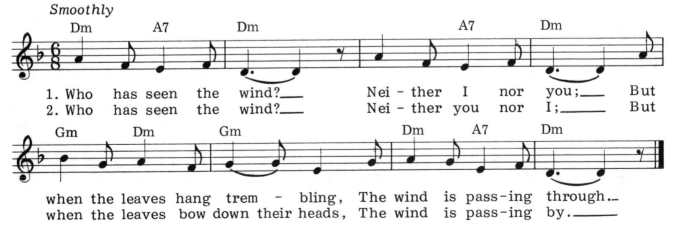

1. Who has seen the wind?___ Nei - ther I nor you;___ But
2. Who has seen the wind?___ Nei - ther you nor I;___ But

when the leaves hang trem - bling, The wind is pass-ing through.___
when the leaves bow down their heads, The wind is pass-ing by. ___

The Wind

Smoothly

1. Wind - mills are turn - ing, turn - ing, turn - ing.

Wind - mills are turn - ing a - round and a - round.

2. Pinwheels are turning, etc.
3. My kite is flying, etc.

From SING AND BE HAPPY by June Norton. Copyright © 1935, 1951, 1963 by June Mary Norton and Charlotte Byj. Published by John Day. Used by permission of Thomas Y. Crowell.

Let's Go Fly a Kite

Cheerfully

Let's go fly a kite, Up to the

high - est height! Let's go fly a kite And

send it soar - ing. Up through the

at - mos - phere, Up where the air is clear.

Oh, let's go _____ fly a kite! _____

Tree in the Woods

3. And on that branch, there was a nest; etc.
4. And in that nest, there was an egg; etc.
5. And in the egg, there was a bird; etc.
6. And on the bird, there was a feather; etc.
7. And from the feather, there was a bed; etc.
8. And on the bed, there was a child; etc.
9. And then the child, he planted a seed; etc.
10. And from that seed, there grew a tree; etc.

Arrangement from MUSIC FOR EARLY CHILDHOOD © 1952 by Silver-Burdett Company.
Used by permission.

St. Patrick's Day

Liltingly

The pip - er plays a lilt - ing air, The chil - dren dance in the vil - lage square, And what is the day that is bring - ing them there? Saint Pat - rick's Day in the morn - ing.

Michael Finnigin

Lively

1. There once was a man named Mi-chael Fin-ni-gin,
He grew whis-kers on his chin-ni-gin, The wind came out and
blew them in-i-gin, Poor old Mi-chael Fin-ni-gin (be-gin-i-gin).

2. There once was a man named Mi-chael Fin-ni-gin,
He kicked up an aw-ful din-i-gin, Be-cause they said he
must not sing-i-gin, Poor old Mi-chael Fin-ni-gin (be-gin-i-gin).

3. There once was a man named Michael
  Finnigin,
  He went fishing with a pinigin,
  Caught a fish but dropped it inigin,
  Poor old Michael Finnigin (beginigin).

4. There once was a man named Michael
  Finnigin,
  Climbed a tree and barked his shinigin,
  Took off several yards of skinigin,
  Poor old Michael Finnigin (beginigin).

5. There once was a man named Michael
  Finnigin,
  He grew fat and he grew thinigin,
  Then he died, and we have to beginigin,
  Poor old Michael Finnigin.

The Easter Bunny

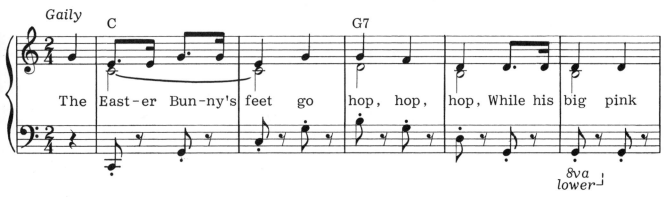

The East-er Bun-ny's feet go hop, hop, hop, While his big pink

8va lower

ears— go— flop, flop, flop, He is rush-ing on his way, For

East-er's a big day, With a hop, flop, hop, flop, hop.

Mister Rabbit

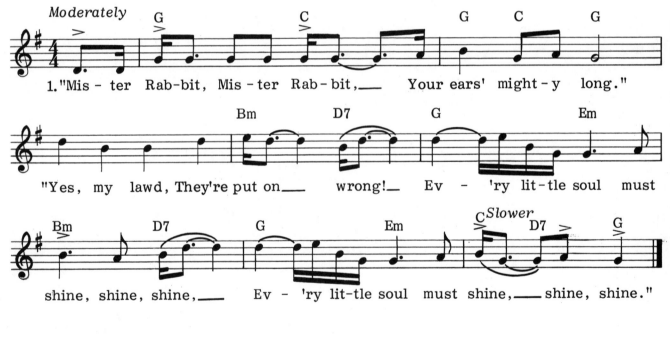

1. "Mis-ter Rab-bit, Mis-ter Rab-bit,___ Your ears' might-y long."
"Yes, my lawd, They're put on___ wrong!___ Ev-'ry lit-tle soul must
shine, shine, shine,___ Ev-'ry lit-tle soul must shine,___ shine, shine."

2. "Mister Rabbit, Mister Rabbit,
   Your coat's mighty gray."
   "Yes, my lawd,
   It was made that way."
   Chorus

3. "Mister Rabbit, Mister Rabbit,
   Your tail's mighty white."
   "Yes, my lawd,
   I'm a-gettin' out of sight!"
   Chorus

From ON THE TRAIL OF NEGRO FOLKSONGS by Dorothy Scarborough, Cambridge, Mass.: Harvard University Press. Copyright © 1925 by Harvard University Press; 1953 by Mary McDaniel Parker. Reprinted by permission of the publishers.

Easter Eggs

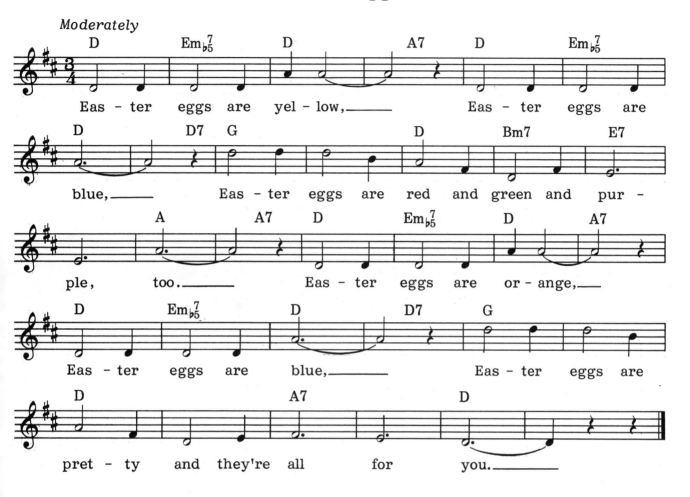

Eas - ter eggs are yel - low,_____ Eas - ter eggs are blue,_____ Eas - ter eggs are red and green and pur - ple, too._____ Eas - ter eggs are or - ange,_____ Eas - ter eggs are blue,_____ Eas - ter eggs are pret - ty and they're all for you._____

From THE SUNFLOWER SONGBOOK by June Norton. Copyright © 1935, 1956, 1963 by June Mary Norton and Charlotte Byj. Published by John Day. Used by permission of Thomas Y. Crowell.

Sally Go Round the Sun

Moderately

Sal - ly go round the sun, Sal - ly go round the moon,

Sal - ly go round the chim - ney top Ev - 'ry af - ter - noon.

Sunshine

Brightly

Sun-shine, sun-shine, peep-ing in our win-dow, Will you come and stay with us and

shine so bright? "Yes," said the sun - shine, peep-ing in our win - dow,

"I will stay all day. I must go home at night."

Transportation

Row, Row, Row Your Boat

Steadily　　　　　　　　　　　　　　　　　　　　　　　　　*Round*

Row, row, row your boat Gent - ly down the stream.__

Mer-ri - ly, mer-ri -ly, mer-ri -ly,mer-ri -ly, Life is but a dream.__

French:
Rame, rame, rame donc.
Vague les canots.
Joliment, joliment, joliment, joliment,
Attaquons le flot.

Riding in My Car

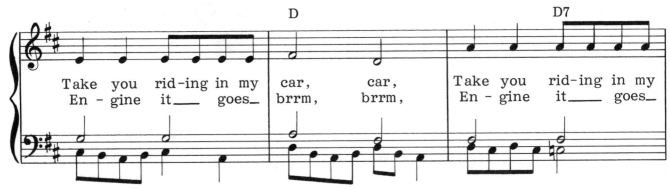

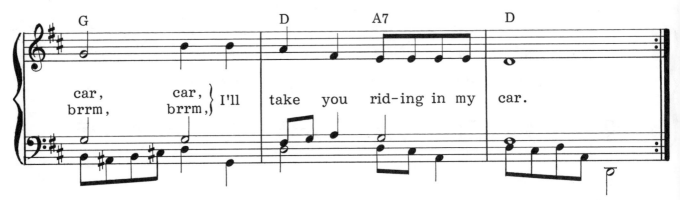

3. Click clack, open up a door, girls,
   Click clack, open up a door, boys,
   Front door, back door, clickety clack,
   Take you riding in my car.

4. Trees and houses walk along,
   Trees and houses walk along,
   Truck and a car, and a garbage can,
   Take you riding in my car.

5. Climb climb, rattle on a front seat,
   Spree I spraddle on a back seat,
   Turn on my key, step on my starter,
   Take you riding in my car.

6. I'm-a gonna roll you home again,
   I'm-a gonna roll you home again,
   Brrm, brrm, chrrka, chrrka, rolly home,
   Take you riding in my car.

7. I'm-a gonna let you blow the horn,
   I'm-a gonna let you blow the horn,
   Oorah, oorahh, oogah, oogahh,
   Take you riding in my car.

8. Brrm, brrm, chrrka, chrrka, brrm, brrm,
   Brrm, brrm, chrrka, chrrka, brrm, brrm,
   Brrm, brrm, chrrka, chrrka, brrm, brrm,
   Take you riding in my car.

The Wheels of the Bus

Rhythmically

1. The wheels_ of the bus_ go_ 'round and 'round,
'round and 'round, 'round and 'round. The wheels_ of the bus_ go_
'round and 'round,_ O - ver the cit - y streets._____

2. The horn on the bus goes toot, toot, toot,
Toot, toot, toot, toot, toot, toot.
The horn on the bus goes toot, toot, toot,
At all the buses it meets.

3. The people on the bus go up and down,
Up and down, up and down.
The people on the bus go up and down,
While bouncing on their seats.

When You Ride a Bicycle

Smoothly

When you ride a bi - cy - cle, Watch out for the mo - tor cars;

When you ride a bi - cy - cle, Nev-er take your hands off the han - dle-bars;

Ped - al slow - ly to and fro, You'll get where you want to go,

Don't do tricks you think you know, 'Cause you saw them at the show;

Keep cool as an i - ci - cle, When you ride a bi - cy - cle.

The Little Red Wagon

Lively

1. Jolt-ing up and down in the lit-tle red wag - on, Jolt-ing up and down in the lit-tle red wag - on, Jolt-ing up and down in the lit-tle red wag - on, Won't you be my dar - ling?

2. Now what's happened to the little red wagon, etc.

3. One wheel's off and the axle's dragging, etc.

Trucks

Vigorously

1. I'll drive a dump truck, I'll drive a dump truck,
I'll drive a dump truck down the street.

2. I'll drive a tow truck, etc.
3. I'll drive a gas truck, etc.

Have children suggest additional verses about other kinds of trucks.

Down by the Station

Moderately

Down by the sta - tion Ear - ly in the morn - ing,

I can see the puff-ing en-gines All in a row. I can see the en-gi-neer

Pull a lit-tle le - ver. Choo! Choo! Wooo! Wooo! Off they go!

I've Been Workin' on the Railroad

Lively

I've been work-in' on the rail - road, All the live - long day;

I've been work-in' on the rail - road, Just to pass the time a - way.

The Train Is A-Comin'

Steadily

1. The train is a-com-in', oh, yes. Train is a-com-in',— oh, yes.

Train is a-com-in', Train is a-com-in', Train is a-com-in', oh, yes.

2. Better get your ticket, oh, yes, etc.
3. Room for many more, etc.
4. (child's name) is the engineer, etc.
5. (child's name) is the coal car, etc.

Make up additional verses using names of children in the class.

Little Red Caboose

Rhythmically

1. Lit-tle red ca-boose, chug, chug, chug. Lit-tle red ca-boose, chug,
2. Lit-tle red ca-boose, chug, chug, chug. Lit-tle red ca-boose, chug,

chug, chug. Lit-tle red ca-boose be-hind the train, train,
chug, chug. Lit-tle red ca-boose be-hind the train, train,

train, train. Smoke stack on its back, back, back, back. Com-ing down the
train, train. Com-ing round the bend, bend, bend, bend. Hang-ing on the

track, track, track, track. Lit-tle red ca-boose be-hind the train.___
end, end, end, end. Lit-tle red ca-boose be-hind the train.

Animals

Barnyard Song

Gaily

1. I had a bird, and the bird pleased me, I fed my bird by yon-der tree;
2. I had a hen, and the hen pleased me, I fed my hen by yon-der tree;

(2.) Hen goes chim-my chuck, chim-my chuck, Bird goes fid-dle-ee-fee.

3. Duck...quack, quack   4. Goose...swishy, swashy
5. Sheep...baa, baa   6. Pig...griffy, griffy
7. Cow...moo, moo   8. Horse...neigh, neigh etc.

Omit the ¾ measure in the first verse and sing it only once in
the second. After the second verse, sing the animal names
and sounds of all the previous verses in reverse order before
going on to: "Bird goes fiddle-ee-fee."

131

Jig Along Home

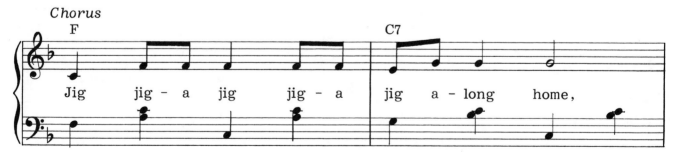

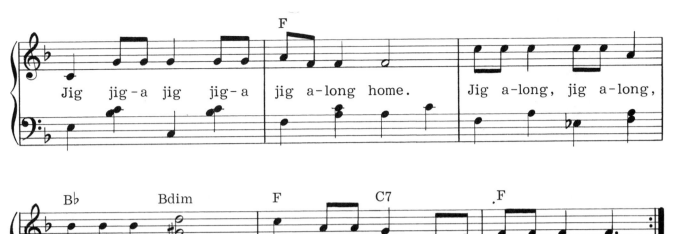

3. Mama rat took off her hat,
   Shook the house with the old tom cat.
   The alligator beat his tail on the drum,
   Jig along, jig along, jig along home.
   Chorus

4. The boards did rattle and the house did shake;
   The clouds did laugh and the world did quake.
   New moon rattled some silver spoons,
   Jig along, jig along, jig along home.
   Chorus

5. The nails flew loose and the floors broke down;
   Everybody danced around and around.
   The house come down and the crowd went
     home,
   Jig along, jig along, jig along home.
   Chorus

I Know an Old Lady

Moderately

I know an old la - dy who swal - lowed a fly. I don't know why she swal-lowed a fly! I guess she'll die!_____ I know an old la - dy who swal - lowed a spi - der that wrig - gled and wrig - gled and tick-led in-side her. She swal-lowed a spi-der to catch the fly, But I don't know why she swal-lowed the fly! I guess she'll die!____ I know an old la - dy who swal-lowed a { bird. Now / cat. Now / dog. My, / goat. Just / cow. }

how ab - surd, to swal - low a bird! She
fan - cy that, to swal - low a cat! She
what a hog, to swal - low a dog! She
o - pened her throat and in walked the goat! She
I don't know how she swal - lowed a cow! She

No repeat first time

(a) swal - lowed the bird to catch the spi - der That
(b) swal - lowed the cat to catch the bird. She *(To a)*
(c) swal - lowed the dog to catch the cat. She *(To b)*
(d) swal - lowed the goat to catch the dog. She *(To c)*
swal - lowed the cow to catch the goat. She *(To d)*

wrig - gled and wrig - gled and tick - led in - side her. She

swal-lowed the spi - der to catch the fly, But I don't know why she

swal-lowed the fly; I guess she'll die!___ I die!___ I

(Spoken)

know an old la-dy who swal-lowed a horse! She's dead, of course!

Six Little Ducks

Rhythmically

1. Six lit-tle ducks that I once knew, Fat ones, skin-ny ones,

fair ones too, But the one lit-tle duck with a feath-er on his back,

He led the oth-ers with his quack, quack, quack! quack, quack, quack,

quack, quack, quack! He led the oth-ers with his quack! quack! quack!

2. Down to the river they all did go,
   With a wibble-wobble, wibble-wobble to and
   fro, etc.

3. Up and down the river they swam all day,
   And their tails wiggle-waggled as they did
   play, etc.

4. Home from the river they all did come,
   With a wibble-wobble, wibble-wobble,
   Hi-ho-hum, etc.

Little White Duck

Words by Walt Whippo.

Music by Bernard Zaritsky.

Simply
Chorus

1. There's a lit - tle white duck sit-ting in the wa - ter A
2. (There's a) lit - tle green frog swim-ming in the wa - ter A

lit-tle white duck do-ing what he ought-er He took a bite of a
lit-tle green frog do-ing what he ought-er He jumped right off of the

li - ly pad Flapped his wings and he
li - ly pad That the lit - tle duck bit and he

said, "I'm glad I'm a lit - tle white duck sit-ting in the wa - ter"
said, "I'm glad I'm a lit - tle green frog swim-ming in the wa - ter"

quack, quack, quack. 2. There's a hoo.
glumph, glumph, glumph. 3. There's a

3. There's a little black bug floating in the water,
   A little black bug doing what he oughter,
   He tickled the frog on the lily pad
   That the little duck bit and he said, "I'm glad
   I'm a little black bug floating on the water,"
   Chirp, chirp, chirp.

4. There's a little red snake lying in the water,
   A little red snake doing what he oughter,
   He frightened the duck and the frog so bad,
   He ate the little bug and he said, "I'm glad
   I'm a little red snake lying in the water,"
   Sss, sss, sss.

5. Now there's nobody left sitting in the water,
   Nobody left doing what he oughter,
   There's nothing left but the lily pad,
   The duck and the frog ran away, it's sad
   That there's nobody left sitting in the water,
   Boo, hoo, hoo.

Bill Grogan's Goat

Cheerfully

1. Bill Gro - gan's goat,   Was   feel - ing
2. Bill grabbed that goat,   By the wool of his

fine,   Ate three red shirts,   Right off the line.
back,   And tied him to,   The rail - road track.

3. That goat he bucked
   With might and main,
   As round the curve
   Came a passenger train.

4. That goat he bucked
   With might and main,
   Coughed up those shirts
   And flagged the train.

From THE FIRESIDE BOOK OF CHILDREN'S SONGS by Marie Winn and Allan Miller. Copyright © 1966 by Marie Winn and Allan Miller. Used by permission of Simon & Schuster, a Division of Gulf & Western Corporation.

The Animal Fair

Bouncing

I went to the an-i-mal fair,____ The birds and the beasts were there,____ The big ba-boon by the light of the moon was comb-ing his au-burn hair.____ The mon-key he got drunk,____ And fell on the el-e-phant's trunk;____ The el-e-phant sneezed and fell on his knees, And that was the end of the monk, the monk, the monk, the monk, the monk. The monk. The monk.

Circus Songs

The Clown

Moderately

Oh, see the clown in his fun-ny hat!

Patch-es on his pants and he's big and fat. Long flap-py shoes and a

round red nose, Makes peo-ple laugh wher-ev-er he goes.

The Elephant

Steadily

See the el-e-phant com-ing by, Flap-ping ears and ti-ny eye.

See him swing-ing his great big trunk As he walks, ka-lunk, ka-lunk, ka-lunk.

The Lion

Brightly

The li-on tam-er cracks his whip, The li-on roars in rage,_____ He
licks his chops so hun-gry-like, I'm glad he's in a cage!_____

The Seal

Moderately

The seal can catch and jug-gle things, He climbs a lad-der and he swings. He
walks on flip-pers, but he's quick. He looks all shin-y, black and slick.

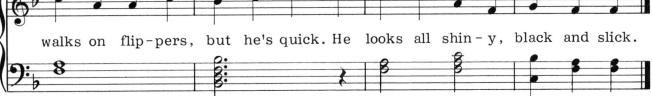

Other Lands

Les Petites Marionnettes

Brightly

French Folk Tune

Chords: F B♭ F C7 F B♭ F C7 F

Ain - si font, font, font, les pe - ti - tes mar - ion - net - tes. Ain - si
See them dance so! so! All the lit - tle mar - ion - net - tes. See them

font, font, font, trois p'tites tours et puis s'en vont!
dance so! so! Three lit - tle turns and off they go!

Frère Jacques

Lightly and politely

French Round

Frè - re Jac-ques, Frè - re Jac-ques, Dor-mez-vous? Dor-mez-vous?

Son-nez les ma-ti-nes, Son-nez les ma-ti-nes, Din, din, don. Din, din, don.

English:
Are you sleeping, are you sleeping,
Brother John, Brother John?
Morning bells are ringing, morning bells are
    ringing,
Ding, ding, dong. Ding, ding, dong.

Spanish:
¿Frey Felipe, Frey Felipe,
Duermes tu, duermes tu?
Tocan las campanas, tocan las campanas,
Tan, tan, tan. Tan, tan, tan.

Yiddish:
Onkel Jakob, Onkel Jakob,
Schläfst du noch, schläfst du noch?
Ringe an der Glocke, ringe an der Glocke,
Bim, bam, bom. Bim, bam, bom.

Alouette

Crisply

French-Canadian singing game

A - lou-et - te, gen-tille A - lou-et - te, A - lou-et - te,

Je te plu - me-rai.

Fine

1. Je te plu - me-rai la tête,
2. Je te plu - me-rai le bec,

Je te plu-me-rai la tête, Et la tête, Et la tête,
Je te plu-me-rai le bec, Et le bec, Et le bec,(to 1) Oh!_____

D.C.

1. *la tête* (the head)   4. *le dos* (the back)
2. *le bec* (the beak)   5. *les pattes* (the feet)
3. *le nez* (the nose)   6. *le cou* (the neck)

Heigh Ho! Anybody Home?

English Round

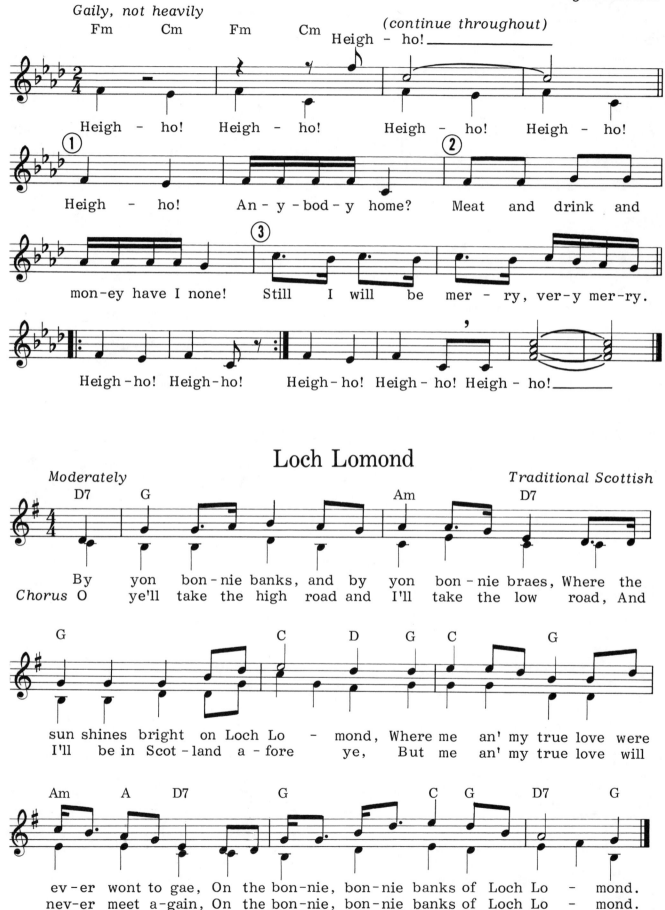

Gaily, not heavily

Heigh - ho! Heigh - ho!

Heigh - ho! Heigh - ho! Heigh - ho! Heigh - ho!

Heigh - ho! An - y-bod-y home? Meat and drink and

mon-ey have I none! Still I will be mer - ry, ver-y mer-ry.

Heigh - ho! Heigh-ho! Heigh-ho! Heigh - ho! Heigh - ho!

Loch Lomond

Moderately

Traditional Scottish

By yon bon - nie banks, and by yon bon - nie braes, Where the
Chorus O ye'll take the high road and I'll take the low road, And

sun shines bright on Loch Lo - mond, Where me an' my true love were
I'll be in Scot - land a - fore ye, But me an' my true love will

ev - er wont to gae, On the bon - nie, bon - nie banks of Loch Lo - mond.
nev - er meet a - gain, On the bon - nie, bon - nie banks of Loch Lo - mond.

144

Sarasponda

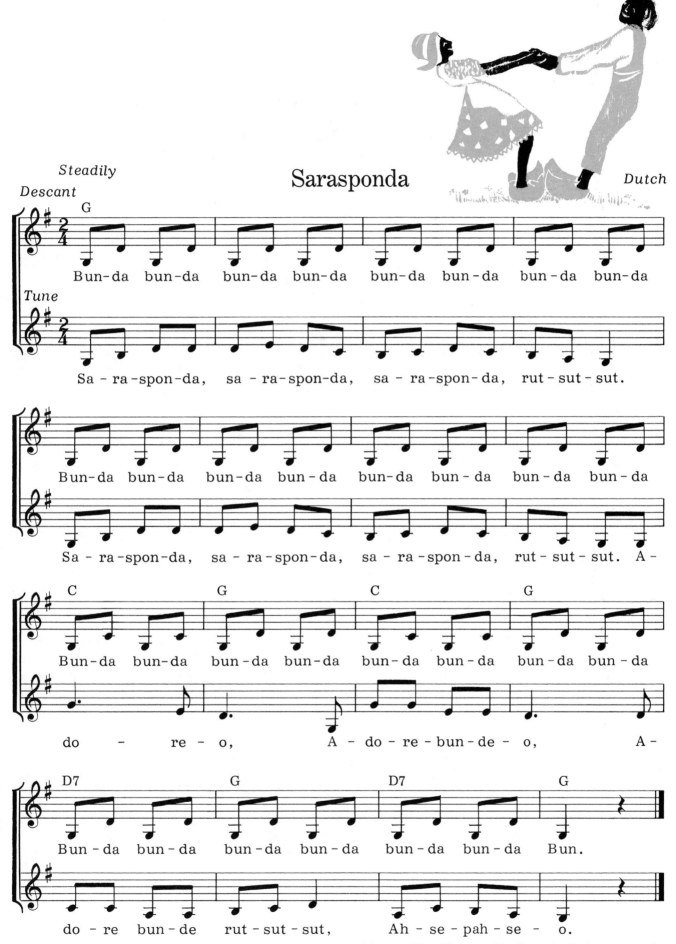

Steadily

Descant

G

Bun-da bun-da bun-da bun-da bun-da bun-da bun-da bun-da

Tune

Sa - ra-spon-da, sa - ra-spon-da, sa - ra-spon-da, rut - sut - sut.

Bun-da bun-da bun-da bun-da bun-da bun-da bun-da bun-da

Sa - ra-spon-da, sa - ra-spon-da, sa - ra-spon-da, rut - sut - sut. A -

C   **G**   **C**   **G**

Bun-da bun-da bun-da bun-da bun-da bun-da bun-da bun-da

do - re - o,   A - do - re - bun - de - o,   A -

D7   **G**   **D7**   **G**

Bun-da bun-da bun-da bun-da bun-da bun-da Bun.

do - re bun - de rut - sut - sut, Ah - se - pah - se - o.

Dutch

Zum Gali Gali

Israeli

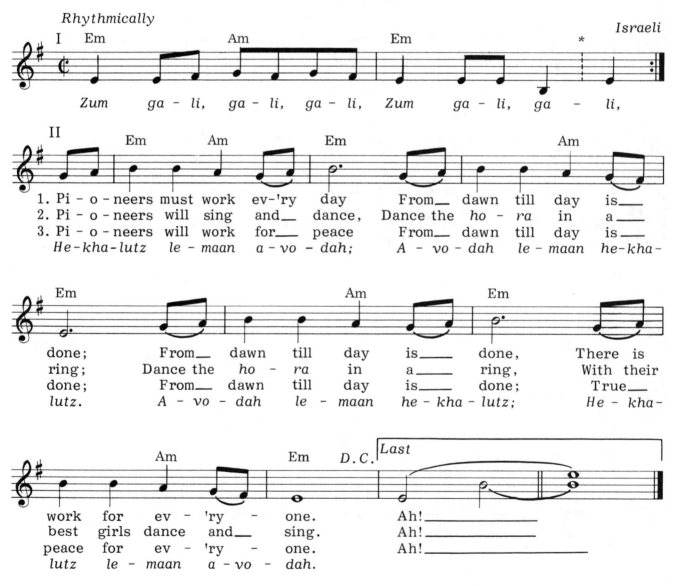

Rhythmically

I Em   Am   Em   *

Zum   ga - li, ga - li, ga - li, Zum   ga - li, ga - li,

II   Em   Am   Em   Am

1. Pi - o - neers must work ev-'ry day   From__ dawn till day is__
2. Pi - o - neers will sing and__ dance, Dance the *ho - ra* in a__
3. Pi - o - neers will work for__ peace   From__ dawn till day is__
He-kha-lutz le - maan a - vo - dah;   A - vo - dah le - maan he-kha-

Em   Am   Em

done;   From__ dawn till day is__ done,   There is
ring;   Dance the *ho - ra* in a__ ring,   With their
done;   From__ dawn till day is__ done;   True__
lutz.   A - vo - dah le - maan he - kha - lutz;   He - kha-

Am   Em   D.C. |Last

work for ev - 'ry - one.   Ah!_____
best girls dance and__ sing. Ah!_____
peace for ev - 'ry - one.   Ah!_____
lutz le - maan a - vo - dah.

* Have Group I sing its part through two times before Group
II begins. Group I will then continue signing its part until
Group II completes all the verses.

Kookaburra

Gaily

**① C   F   C   **

1. Koo - ka - bur - ra sits   in the old gum tree,_____
2. Koo - ka - bur - ra sits   in the old gum tree,_____

②   F   C

Mer - ry, mer - ry king   of the bush is he,_____
Eat - ing all the gum - drops he can see,_____

③   F   C

Laugh,   Koo - ka bur - ra, laugh,   Koo - ka - bur - ra,
Stop,   Koo - ka bur - ra, stop,   Koo - ka - bur - ra,

④   F   C

Gay   your   life   must   be.
Leave   some   there   for   me.

From *The Ditty Bag*, compiled by Janet E. Tobbitt.

Mexican Hat Dance

sombrero (hat)
maracas (rattles)
claves (hardwood sticks)

Mexican Folk Tune

We will dance all a-round the som - bre - ro, Tra la
la la la la la la la la, We will dance all a-round the som-
bre - ro, Tra la la la la la la la la._____
We will shake_and shake our ma - ra-cas, (shake maracas) And we'll
tap_ and tap on our cla - ves, (tap on claves)

From William R. Sur, Adeline McCall, William R. Fisher, and Mary R. Tolbert, THIS IS MUSIC, BOOK I. Copyright © 1967 by Allyn & Bacon, Inc., Boston. Reprinted with permission.

La Cucaracha

Brightly

Mexican Folk Tune

1. When they dance the *cu-ca-ra-cha*, And I hear the mu-sic play-ing,

To the Pla-za then I hur-ry, Join the dance with-out de-lay-ing, *La cu-ca-*

ra - cha, La-cu-ca-ra - cha, Ya no pue-de cam-i - nar, Por-que no

tien - e, Por-que le fal - tan, Las dos pa - ti -tas de atrás.

Day, Dah Light
(*The Banana-Boat Loaders' Song*)

Day, O!__ Day,__ O!__ Day, dah light__ break,__ me

wan' go home.__ Come, Mis-sa Tal-ly man, come
Come here for work__ did-n't

tal-ly me ba-nan-a,)
come here for to i-dle,)
Day, dah light__ break,__ me wan' go home.__

Everybody Loves Saturday Night

Brightly

African Folk Tune

(English) 1. Ev - 'ry - bod - y loves Sat - ur - day night,_____

(French) 2. Tout le monde aime Sam - e - di soir,_____

Ev - 'ry - bod - y loves Sat - ur - day

Tout le monde aime Sam - e - di

night,_____ Ev - 'ry - bod - y,

soir,_____ Tout le monde aime,

Ev - 'ry - bod - y, Ev - 'ry - bod - y, Ev - 'ry - bod - y,

Tout le monde aime, Tout le monde aime, Tout le monde aime,

Ev - 'ry - bod - y loves Sat - ur - day night._____

Tout le monde aime Sam - e - di soir._____

German:

Eider man hat dem Samstag Abend,
Eider man hat dem Samstag Abend,
Eider man hat, Eider man hat,
Eider man hat, Eider man hat,
Eider man hat dem Samstag Abend.

Italian:

Tutti ama Sabato sera,
Tutti ama Sabato sera,
Tutti ama, Tutti ama,
Tutti ama, Tutti ama,
Tutti ama Sabato sera.

Spanish:

El Sábado ama todo el mundo,
El Sábado ama todo el mundo,
Todo el mundo, Todo el mundo,
Todo el mundo, Todo el mundo,
El Sábado ama todo el mundo.

Yiddish:

Yeder ener glächt Shabbas ba nacht,
Yeder ener glächt Shabbas ba nacht,
Yeder ener, Yeder ener,
Yeder ener, Yeder ener,
Yeder ener glächt Shabbas ba nacht.

Chapter headings appear in **bold** type, song
titles in CAPITALS, and first lines in *italics*.